CARRERE
CBS
BARBRA & NEIL
MILK & HONEY
HALLELUJAH
Israelische Inzending Eurovisie Songfestival 1979
Polydor
45
STEREO
Y.M.C.A.
VILLAGE PEOPLE
THE V
It's Raining
Messing Shoe Blues
Rainbo
Guys 'n' Dolls
's Smile)
ALICIA BRIDGES
Polydor
45

Enjoy reading to Tunes?

Scan the **QR CODE** below for a gnarly playlist curated to accompany this bodacious issue of the Magpie Messenger.

TABLE OF CONTENTS

SPRING 2023

STORIES

Meet the Unkindness

Curious Corvid Publishing is a group effort. The amazing content we're able to bring to you is thanks to the tireless efforts of our team of editors, artists, and the fearless leadership of our founder, Ravven.

RAVVEN WHITE

FOUNDER

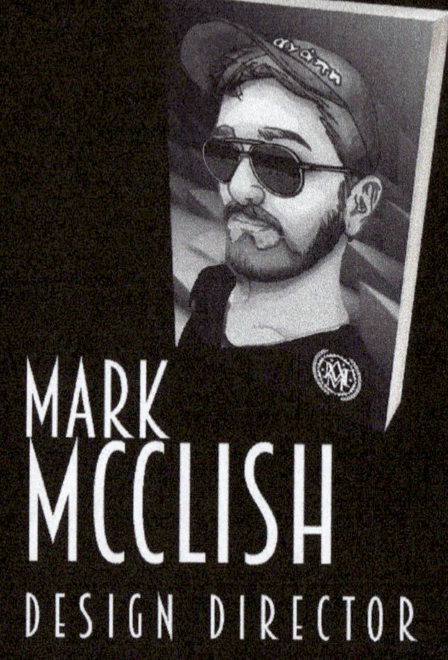

MARK MCCLISH

DESIGN DIRECTOR

ALEXANDRIA YALE

SECRETARY

ANNA CORBEAUX

EDITOR IN CHIEF

JESSICA WELLS

COPY EDITOR

AIMEE NICOLE

COPY EDITOR

Let us recommend
a book for you!

Scenes from your childhood

Corey Bryan

The sun was fixed in the sky like a fugitive in an orange jumpsuit radiating anger.

The evergreen forest was
shedding to carpet the
steeled winter earth.
pinecones and needles in a
mosaic of brown and green.
The swing set sat neglected,
chains rusted, slack like
abandoned moorings.

It creaked under the
stress of your weight,
unsure of itself.
its chains, yawning
after years of
hibernation, start to
sway, back and forth,
picking up speed and
confidence.

In a flash you're off the swing, gliding through thick, wet
air to land on your hands and knees in the mulch.

The intractable wood opens the soft flesh of your palms.
The strawberry red blood glistens in the late Sunday light.

A dog barks indifferently
at the sun as it sheds its
cumbersome bonds and
falls back into the earth.

©2023 Corey Bryan. Used with permission.

Corey Bryan

is a fourth year student at Georgia State University majoring in Rhetoric and Composition. He is currently writing daily poetry prompts, along with some original poems, with a friend of his at poetryispretentious.com. He lives in Atlanta, Georgia with his 3 beautiful cats and wonderful girlfriend, Sarah.

1
Upcoming events for
—
Curious Corvid Publishing
—
In 2023

1
SIDE

April

The Ghoulish Book Festival
San Antonio, Texas
April 14th–16th, 2023

Come and see Ravven White, Grace R.
Reynolds, Michael Perret, and many more
talented dark authors at this incredible
ghoulish event!

1

The L.A. Times Festival of Books
Los Angeles, California
April 22nd–23rd, 2023
—
This is the largest book festival in the United
States and showcases presses and authors
from all across the U.S.! Come see Ravven
and Adanna, the Writer's and Publisher's
Network and a host of other talented authors!

BOOKERY

The full launch of our brand new indie ebook platform is scheduled for early April! It will be the place for indie books, reviews, and social activity. Prepare yourself for a new age in indie reading. Indie Ebooks. Better.

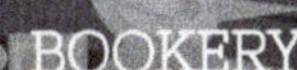

APRIL

Grace R. Reynolds is releasing her second poetry collection, The Lies We Weave. This gut-wrenching new collection highlights womanhood, motherhood, and healing generational trauma.

Closing out poetry month is Anne Marie Wells and her debut collection, Survived By. Telling the story of losing her father to cancer, Survived By is a candid look at grief when life must continue to go on.

MAY

Ravven White has a brand new gothic poetry collection arriving titled Haunted Whispers From A Forgotten Castle. Is it madness or is it misery?

JUNE

The Jersey Devil comes to town in a thrilling new novel from R. E. Sohl. We love a cryptid and this one will thrill you to your core!

JUNE

Join us for a live interview with Robert as we discuss his books, the writing life and whatever else comes up. Robert is an incredible author of the odd and unusual and talking with him always makes for a good time!

JULY

The weather is hot and so are fated prophecies. The Legend of Chaos saga continues with Rey Wicks' *City of Thieves.* Will Sebastion reclaim his birthright? Or will he succumb to the darkness within?

Stay up to date with Curious Corvid events
by following us on Instagram or joining our Discord server!

AN ADVENTURE THROUGH DISBELIEF

By Drew Campbell

Time strides,

Wasted,

As sides switch.

The only constant,

Is opposition.

There is safety,

With the underdog.

Those who sail too far,

Often set their moods to gloom.

Harsh bites,

Reflexes to concern.

The inability to temper,

A need to rewind.

When symbols were treasures.

An aura encasing,

Suspension in time.

Progress woven around,

Spools, with repetition.

Metals heat,

As it features in circles.

Crisp resolution,

Reminds me of static.

The days spent inside fragile curations.

An adventure through disbelief.

Feelings wrapped in mylar.

An unimpeded shell,

Impervious to cracks.

But only from the inside…

Drew Campbell is a writer & artist from California.
Together with his partner, he runs VLASINDA PRODUCTIONS. Their focus is on creating artwork in multiple mediums, as well as organizing events and platforms to help other creatives network and showcase their work. Recently Vlasinda launched BROKEN GALAXIES MAGAZINE, a zine series featuring creators from around the world who write and draw within the genres of Science Fiction, Horror, and Fantasy. For more information and updates, visit IG: @vlasinda_stormdrain & YouTube.com/vlaSINda

Arcade

ICEBALL FX
YOUR SCORE
0
ICEBALL FX
YOUR SCORE
0
ICEBALL FX
YOUR SCORE
00
10.000
3.000
2.000
1.000

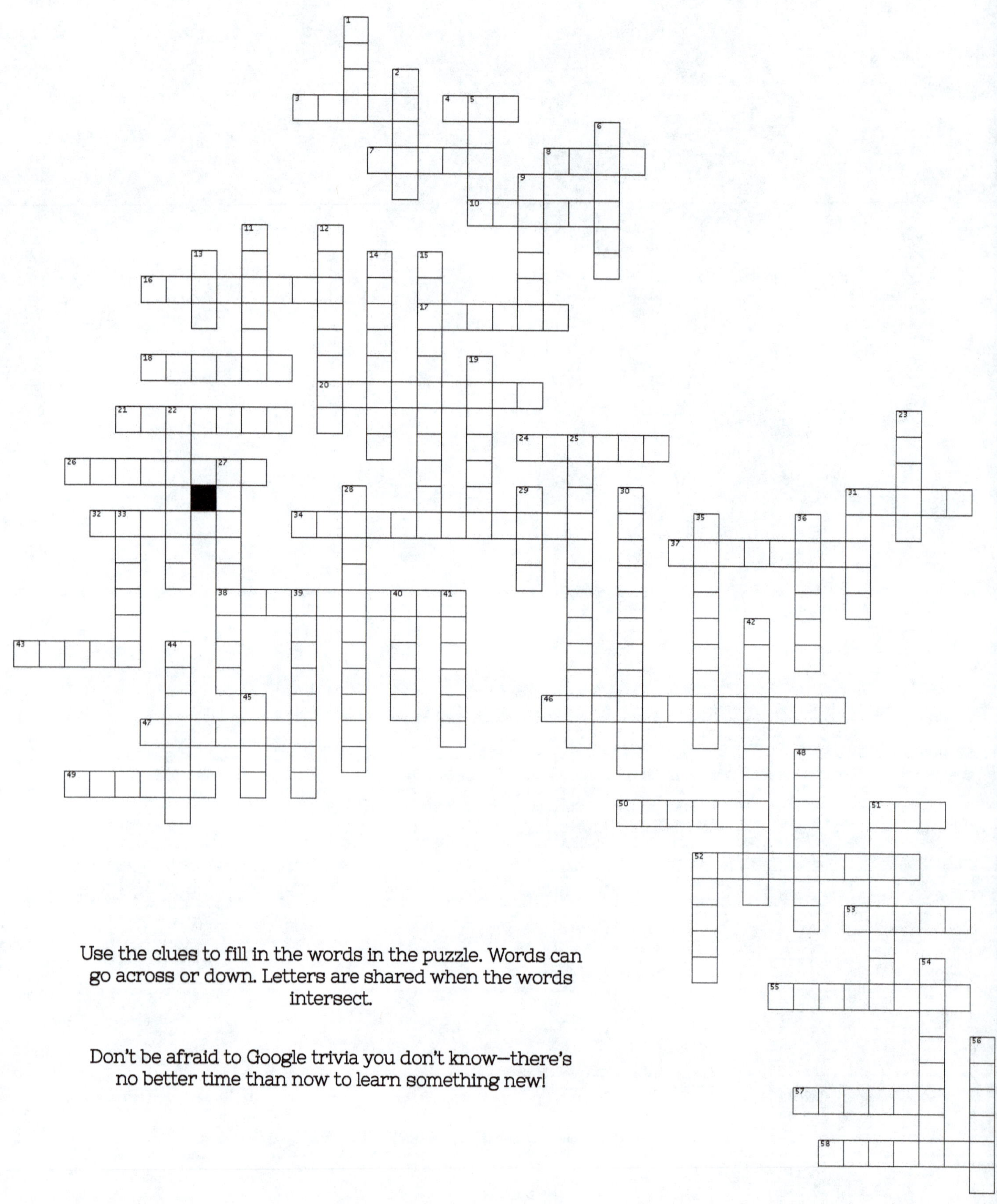

Use the clues to fill in the words in the puzzle. Words can go across or down. Letters are shared when the words intersect.

Don't be afraid to Google trivia you don't know—there's no better time than now to learn something new!

ACROSS

3. "It's dangerous to go alone! Take this."
4. Be kind; rewind
7. The People's Princess
8. 80s eyeshadow shade
10. Hands Across America founder
16. We're living in a _ _ _ _ _ _ _ _ world
17. Business in the front and party in the back
18. Just Say No program launcher
20. 80s TV detective show in the 80s
21. Strike pins to win
24. Underwater city
26. Book festival in San Antonio
31. 867-5309
32. Low crotch pants
34. Our ARC program partner
37. Saturday morning is for watching
38. Shuttle launch disaster
43. Work Out With Jane _ _ _ _ _
46. 80s street dance
47. He feeds Audrey II
49. Guardian Angel author:
50. Colorful cube puzzle
51. One Last Caress protagonist
52. Soviet nuclear disaster
53. I would walk 500
55. Most popular 1982 album
57. Don't forget your quarters
58. Iceberg sank it

Puzzle answers in next issue.

DOWN

1. 80s shopping center
2. His princess is in another castle
5. First heart transplant patient
6. Star of 24-hr news
9. Ultimate indie magazine
11. Confirmation Day author
12. First African-American Miss America
13. Launched August 1st, 1981
14. Three strikes you're out!
15. Beware the stare of
19. Physical playlist for your crush
22. The OG personal music player
23. "Belt Bag"
25. No Dana only Zuul
27. 80s hair tie
28. First cable for children
29. 80s bright glow
30. Nuisance added to cable in 1980
31. Hockey mask slasher
33. I bless the rains
35. Secret to 'big hair'
36. Tom Cruise breakout role
39. Popular aerobics attire
40. 80s often referred to as the decade of:
41. THE 80s sunglasses
42. Beloved movie renter
44. Handheld video game
45. Soda originally with drugs
48. Queen of MTV
51. 1981 most popular song
52. Ready Player One author
54. Time machine car
56. 1988 Microsoft software suite

Guardian
Angel

Guardian Angel

By Kevin Hopson

————

"Liam."

I spun around to look, and a portly fellow with thinning blond hair stared back at me. His name was Charles, and he was a frequent drinker at the bar.

It was a small room with ten stools at the counter, about a dozen tables in the main seating area, a pool table situated in one corner, and several neon beer signs adorning the far wall. But it was a slow evening with only a few customers scattered about.

"Yeah," I said.

"Do you mind turning up the game?"

It was 1986 and the New York Mets were playing the Boston Red Sox in the World Series. I pivoted toward the television, which rested on a makeshift shelf in the corner, and put a hand to the volume knob, gradually turning it.

"Thanks," Charles said.

"Sure. Can I get you anything else?"

"I'm good," he said, taking a drag from his cigarette. "Thanks."

Chatter from a nearby table caught my attention, and I watched as Charles glanced over his shoulder.

"I wish those two would keep it down," he said.

I glimpsed the man and the woman at the table. They were in a heated discussion, but the man was dishing it out more than the woman. The man was bald and sported a mustache, and he appeared to be a little flabby in the belly.

Charles caught me eyeing them.

"Want me to say something?" he said.

I noticed the man rise from the table, heading to the rear of the bar where the restrooms were.

"No," I said. "I'll take care of it."

I circled the counter and walked toward the table, the woman meeting my gaze as I approached.

"Is everything okay?" I asked, stopping beside her.

She had chestnut hair, which rested along her shoulders, and matching brown eyes. The woman sniffled.

"I'm sorry," she finally said. "I know we're being loud."

"But are you okay?" I reiterated.

She eventually nodded. "Yeah. He has a temper, though."

That much was obvious.

"What's your name?" I asked.

"Danielle."

"Well, Danielle. If you feel threatened or scared, order an Angel Lover from Katie."

Katie was the woman serving their table.

"What's an Angel Lover?" Danielle said.

"It's not a real drink," I answered. "It's just a code word. A signal for me to intervene," I elaborated.

A slight grin stretched across her face. "I appreciate that."

"No problem. Can I get you anything?"

"No, but thank you."

Content for the time being, I made my way behind the counter again.

"She okay?" Charles asked.

I shrugged.

Charles took a sip from his glass, turning his attention to the game. "Jesus. The Mets are going to blow this."

I eyed the Zenith television. The Mets were down 3-2 in the best-of-seven series, and they were trailing by two runs in the bottom of the tenth inning. There were two outs and no one on base. I think Charles was right. The Mets were about to blow it.

A few minutes passed, and I was interrupted by a female voice.

"Liam," Katie said. "The woman at table six just ordered an Angel Lover."

That was Danielle's table, and I noticed her verbal assaulter was back. He was keeping his voice down, but I could see him berating her through clenched teeth.

"Get Nathan," I said to Katie.

Nathan was one of our

bouncers. He was a tall, burly guy with spiky blond hair. Katie disappeared, soon reemerging with Nathan at her side. She split off from Nathan, and Nathan approached Danielle's table. He had words with Danielle, though I couldn't make out what was being said. Danielle eventually stood, and Nathan turned to escort her from the table.

"What the hell?" the temperamental man said, getting to his feet.

That was my cue. I made my way over to the table, the three of them eyeing me as I neared.

"Walk her to her car," I said to Nathan.

He nodded and headed for the door with Danielle. I was a big guy. About six-two and over two hundred pounds, but the guy glaring at me was even bigger. I swallowed and let out a breath.

"You're going to have to leave," I said, attempting to keep my voice steady. "Once the lady is gone, that is."

"This is crap. I didn't do anything wrong."

"You were scaring the woman, and she asked us to intervene."

The man's brow furrowed. Then his eyes widened. "The drink she ordered. I should have known."

He tried to brush by me, but I held my ground.

"Listen, asshole," he said.

He reached a hand into his pocket, and I immediately took a step back. Was he going to pull a knife from his pocket or, worse yet, a gun?

"I'm a cop," the man said, displaying his badge.

I squinted at him. "What?"

"Yeah."

I took a moment to ponder. "Even so, it doesn't give you the right to threaten her."

"It was an act. I'm undercover. She was about to sell me some drugs." The man huffed. "And now she's going to walk free because of you."

The man pushed his way past me, and this time I allowed him to go. I followed on his heels, exiting the bar right behind him. It was dark outside. A brisk breeze tugged at a bead of sweat along my forehead, a shiver escaping me. I noticed a car drive off, and Nathan approached.

"She's on her way home," Nathan said.

"That's great," the cop shouted. "I hope you two are proud of yourselves." He stormed off in the direction of his car.

"What an ass," Nathan murmured to me. He went back inside the bar, leaving me with my thoughts.

I tried to convince myself that I'd done the right thing based on the situation. How could I have known that Danielle was a drug dealer and the man was a cop? Assuming the man was telling the truth. I didn't really get a good look at the badge.

It could have been a fake for all I know. Still, I couldn't shake the guilt that was coursing through me.

When I entered the bar, I was surprised to see Charles standing and cheering.

"The Mets just won," he said, pumping a fist in the air and smiling at me.

Well, at least something had gone right. In fact, the Mets ended up winning the World Series two days later.

By that time, the pang of guilt I felt had started to fade. So, instead of fretting about it, I decided to join in the city's celebration.

©2023 Kevin Hopson. Used with permission.

Kevin has dabbled in many genres over the years. A few of his stories have been contest/award winners, and Kevin's work has appeared in more than twenty anthologies.

Every gemstone needs a little polish

by someone who knows how to bring out the shine

Corbeaux Editorial Services

**Thorough and thoughtful
fiction editing
for dark and paranormal
romance authors**

Proud partner of
Curious Corvid Publishing

corbeauxeditorialservices.com
anna@corbeauxeditorialservices.com

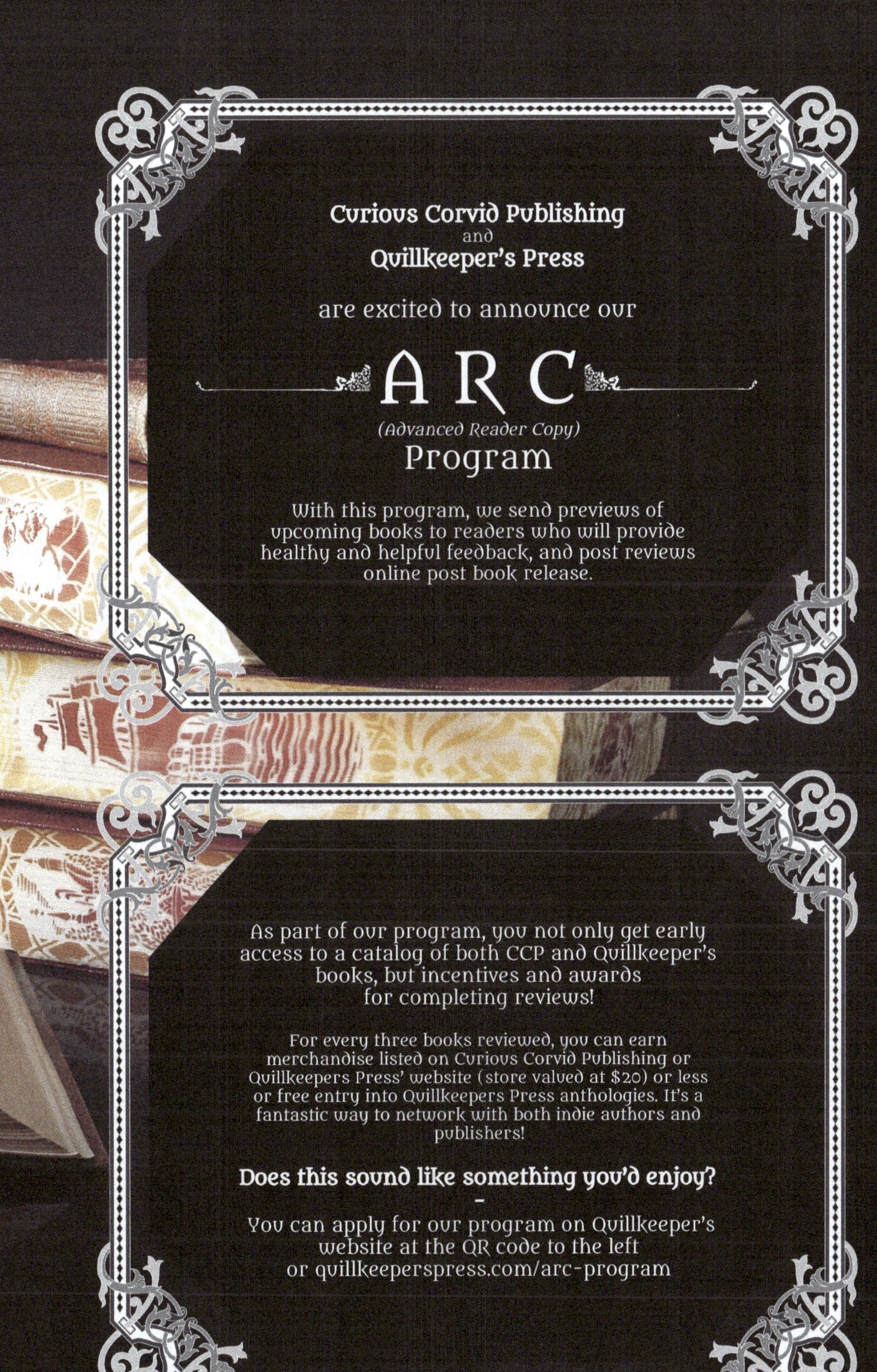

Curious Corvid Publishing
and
Quillkeeper's Press

are excited to announce our

A R C

(Advanced Reader Copy)
Program

With this program, we send previews of
upcoming books to readers who will provide
healthy and helpful feedback, and post reviews
online post book release.

As part of our program, you not only get early
access to a catalog of both CCP and Quillkeeper's
books, but incentives and awards
for completing reviews!

For every three books reviewed, you can earn
merchandise listed on Curious Corvid Publishing or
Quillkeepers Press' website (store valued at $20) or less
or free entry into Quillkeepers Press anthologies. It's a
fantastic way to network with both indie authors and
publishers!

Does this sound like something you'd enjoy?
-
You can apply for our program on Quillkeeper's
website at the QR code to the left
or quillkeeperspress.com/arc-program

THE LEGEND OF RAVVEN

PRESS START BUTTON

I think it's always interesting to learn what people have taken with them from their childhood, especially from folks in the creative community. There's always at least one thing that was super impactful that has transcended time and brings us back to a time of childhood innocence and nostalgia no matter how old we are. Sometimes it's even surprising!

For me, it was a map. Specifically, the map to the *Legend of Zelda* gold edition for the original Nintendo NES. I thought it was the coolest thing in the whole world. I didn't know about companion or play through guides so having this cool foldable map of Link's world was groundbreaking to my ten year old mind. My love of and dedication to the *Legend of Zelda* was solidified that day and nothing will ever quite beat finding your sword as the mysterious old man says to you: "It's dangerous to go alone! Take this!" Sometimes in the morning when we're on our way to work I'll jokingly hand my husband his coffee and remind him that it's dangerous to go alone.

If you're not familiar with *The Legend of Zelda*, here's a little overview:

A small kingdom in the land of Hyrule is engulfed by chaos when an army led by Ganon, the prince of darkness, invaded and stole the Triforce of Power, one part of a magical artifact which alone bestows great strength. In an attempt to prevent him from acquiring the Triforce of Wisdom, Princess Zelda splits it into eight fragments and hides them in secret underground dungeons. Before eventually being kidnapped by Ganon, she commands her nursemaid Impa to find someone courageous enough to save the kingdom. While wandering the land, the old woman is surrounded by Ganon's henchmen, when a young boy named Link appears and rescues her. Upon hearing Impa's plea, he resolves to save Zelda and sets out to reassemble the scattered fragments of the Triforce of Wisdom, with which Ganon can then be defeated.

During the course of the tale, Link locates and braves the eight underworld labyrinths, and beyond their defeated guardian monsters retrieves each fragment. With the completed Triforce of Wisdom, he is able to infiltrate Ganon's hideout in Death Mountain, confronting the prince of darkness and destroying him with the Silver Arrow. Obtaining the Triforce of Power from Ganon's ashes, Link returns it and the restored Triforce of Wisdom to the rescued Princess Zelda, and peace returns to Hyrule.

But back to the map.

The Legend of Zelda also happened to be my dad's favorite game as well. My mom told me that she'd spend hours watching him play and they would draw out maps together as he unlocked new areas. It was a special time for them together and something that they bonded over. My dad unfortunately passed away just before I was born so I never got the opportunity to know him. But knowing the stories of mapmaking and having my own foldable map felt like a bridge between worlds and I felt oddly closer to my gamer father.

The story of Link, an adventure fulfilling his destiny of saving the world and saving the princess was something that resonated deeply with me. I loved and longed for the idea of fighting the monsters and bad guys, exploring new places, and fixing what was wrong. Plus, Link was a little cheeky what with all the pot breaking...It was a game I returned to over and over because it felt like I was writing the story every time I played. Where would I go this time? Which cave would I explore? Which boss would I defeat? Sometimes I ended up in areas that were way beyond my skill level, and I'd be forced to make a hasty retreat for fearing of losing all my hearts.

The Legend of Zelda was my first introduction to action, adventure role playing games. You met fun and interesting characters and your choices determined the speed and outcome of the game. If you were hasty, you missed important things or hidden treasures. It required patience and observation and strong thumbs to swing the sword or run away.

This wasn't the only game that captivated my interest though. *Super Mario Bros.* was another of my favorites which I'm sure many of our readers can agree with. It's become a much beloved series since it's release with spin offs and sequels out the wazoo.

But if anyone here is unfamiliar with *Super Mario Bros*, here's also a brief summary:

In the fantasy setting of the Mushroom Kingdom, a tribe of turtle-like creatures known as the Koopa Troopas invade the kingdom and uses the magic of its king, Bowser, to turn its inhabitants, known as the Mushroom People, into inanimate objects such as bricks, stones and horsehair plants. Bowser and his army also kidnap Princess Toadstool, the princess of the Mushroom Kingdom and the only one with the ability to reverse Bowser's spell. After hearing the news, Mario sets out to save the princess and free the kingdom from Bowser. After traveling through various parts of the kingdom and fighting Bowser's forces along the way, Mario reaches Bowser's final stronghold, where he is able to defeat him by striking an axe on the bridge suspended over lava he is standing on, breaking the bridge, defeating Bowser, freeing the princess and saving the Mushroom Kingdom.

Did you know that Princess Peach's full name was Princess Peach Toadstool?

I think these video games really helped develop my appreciation and love of storytelling as well as teaching me that storytelling can be done in more ways than one. It was a relief to load the games up and disappear into the land of Zelda for a bit, working through the map and looking for the secrets. My love for gaming has continued into adulthood with my husband fondly nicknamed 'Link' a healthy steam collection of games. It's something I have always enjoyed and used as a have when the world gets to be too much.

Sometimes even when I'm writing I find myself reading passages and finding little bits of my childhood gaming leaking through. Situations and characters that remind me of the soft and quiet days of my youth. There's this thing about healing and hearing your inner child and for me, video games will always be apart of that. There's often this stigma that successful and professional adults must eventually hang up the proverbial joystick. We must join the real world, with the real people, and the real jobs.

And while yes, we must unfortunately deal with the world and it's many, many issues, I think it's a bit silly to give up something that gives you that desperately needed drop of serotonin.

Now, video games have become something I share with my husband and with my friends. It's a release and also a social outlet as games like WoW and Final Fantasy bring people together from all over the world. I've talked with people in Australia and Japan – a far cry from my humble little Nintendo.

I'm grateful I was able to experience video games back in the early nineties. It's incredibly cool to see where video games are today and how much they've grown and changed.

Just as I have.

From a little nerd to a grown nerd, there will always be a special place in my heart for *The Legend of Zelda* and *Super Mario Bros.*

And one more thing before you go—

IT'S DANGEROUS TO GO ALONE! TAKE THIS.

The Map, as
mentioned.

Ingredients:

1 medium carrot, coarsely chopped
1 rib celery, coarsely chopped
½ medium onion, coarsely chopped
½ medium red bell pepper, coarsely chopped
4 white mushrooms, coarsely chopped
3 cloves garlic, coarsely chopped
2 ½ pounds ground chuck
1 tablespoon Worcestershire sauce
1 large egg, beaten
1 teaspoon dried Italian herbs
2 teaspoons salt
1 teaspoon ground black pepper
½ teaspoon cayenne pepper
1 cup plain bread crumbs

Glaze Ingredients:
2 tablespoons brown sugar
2 tablespoons ketchup
2 tablespoons Dijon mustard
1 teaspoon Sriracha sauce, or to taste

Directions:

- Preheat the oven to 325°F (165°C). Line a baking dish with lightly greased foil.

- Place carrot, celery, onion, bell pepper, mushrooms, and garlic in a food processor; pulse until very finely chopped, almost to a purée. Transfer to a large mixing bowl. Add ground chuck to the vegetables, along with Worcestershire sauce, egg, Italian herbs, salt, black pepper, and cayenne. Mix gently with a wooden spoon until ingredients are just combined. Sprinkle in bread crumbs and gently mix with your fingertips until just combined; don't overmix.

- Shape the mixture into a loaf, about 4 inches high by 6 inches across. Place in the prepared baking pan. Bake in the preheated oven just until the meatloaf is hot, about 15 minutes.

- Meanwhile, stir brown sugar, ketchup, Dijon, and Sriracha for glaze in a small bowl until brown sugar has dissolved.

- Remove meatloaf from the oven. Spoon glaze on the top of the meatloaf with the back of a spoon, then pull a tiny bit glaze down the sides. Return to the oven, and bake until no longer pink inside, 45 to 75 more minutes. An instant-read thermometer inserted into the thickest part of the loaf should read at least 160°F (70°C), so start checking at 45 minutes and continue baking until meatloaf reaches that temperature. Cooking time will depend on shape and thickness of the meatloaf.

Confirmation Day

Emily Ruth Verona

"sweating like the devil in church,"

…but Ruby Owens is certain the devil has nothing on her in this church on this day. She can already feel perspiration sticky between her armpits as everyone files up to receive the little wafer and a sip of wine. Ruby doesn't budge, except to shift a high-heeled pump across the floor. She knew people dressed up for confirmations, but why had she let her mother talk her into these shoes? They're ridiculous, even if they do make her feel as tall as Gennie. Genevieve O'Reilly is the tallest thirteen-year-old Ruby knows. Has ever known. That's how they met. Gennie was the tallest girl in their homeroom class, Ruby the shortest. They both stuck out and pretty soon they found themselves sticking together. So much so that Ruby now found herself to be the only Jewish kid at Gennie's confirmation.

Saturday morning services at Temple Petah Tikva are usually an all-morning affair, but even with the extra ceremony today the Saint Joseph's mass clocks in at about an hour and ten minutes. Not bad. And the architecture—Ruby hadn't realized it would be so pretty with beautiful, dramatic arches stretched across the ceiling. The kind that keeps you staring long after all the prayers have been said and hymns have been sung, which is exactly what happens. Failing to notice the service's conclusion and the exodus to the rec room for refreshments, Ruby sits in her empty pew counting stained glass windows.

"Ruby Tuesday!" comes a cry as the double doors to the sanctuary swing open. All dressed up in a pretty lavender dress with her dark hair curled in ringlets, Gennie looks like a queen. "How *dare* you leave me alone with those people!"

Ruby smirks. "You mean your parents?"

"Psychopaths! Both of them!" declares Gennie. The elegance of the sanctuary doesn't distract Gennie the way it distracts her less accustomed friend, who takes a moment to pull her thoughts together. Gennie comes and takes a seat next to Ruby. "Were you nervous?" she asks.

Ruby knocks her too-high heels together, the clunky clicking of them echoing across the pews. "Shouldn't I be asking you that?"

"You looked weird after the Eucharist."

"Yeah, well…everyone knew what they were doing and I…I don't know anything about churches. Like, *that*," she gestures to the front of the room. "What do you call that? The bimah looking thing?"

"What's a bimah?"

"Exactly! See, you'd be just as weird with Jewish stuff as I am with Catholic stuff. I mean the platform stagey area…"

"The pulpit?"

Ruby scans the room and points across the aisle to what looks like the fanciest photo booth she's ever seen, with dark wood paneling and red velvet curtains. "And that?"

"Confessional."

"What's it for?"

"Confessing."

"To what? Murder?"

"Your sins. It's pretty much the whole point. If we didn't sin then we wouldn't need to repent, would we?"

Ruby's gaze returns to the confessional, which suddenly possesses the allure of a funhouse. She hates funhouses. "What counts as a sin?"

"Anything you'd get in trouble for. Lying to your parents or wishing Allison Winters would fall down an elevator shaft because she keeps copying your history tests."

"And you tell God? Wouldn't God already know?"

"You tell the priest. There are two stalls, one for the priest and the one for the rest of us. He goes in his side and listens to us talk on our side." Gennie's eyes glitter suddenly, fireworks erupting over a dark night sky. "*Want to see it?*"

"*No!*"

"Why not?"

"Won't I…burst into flames or something?"

Gennie slips her hand into Ruby's clammy palm, pulling her to her feet. "If you burst into flames, I will do your math homework for a month. Besides, it's not your church, so if anyone is going to get in trouble it's me. I'm the one who should know better."

This logic does nothing to reassure Ruby, who already feels herself beginning to sweat again, but that doesn't stop Gennie from dragging her across the sanctuary. Up close, those red curtains are beautiful, reminding Ruby of the soft velvet mantle covering the Torah at her temple.

Gennie grins. "Want to be the priest or the sinner?"

"Neither."

"I'll be the priest then. I've never been a priest before."

Before Ruby can stop her, Gennie disappears behind the velvet curtain on the right and Ruby, not wanting to be caught loitering outside the confessional alone, draws back the curtain on the left and steps inside.

The booth is darker than she'd thought it would be. There's no lamp or anything, just a small bench to sit on and a grated screen in the wall. Light peeks in from the edges of the curtain, but beyond that the space is dim, confining and disorienting. "Can we get out now?" she asks, shouting into the screen like it's the order box at a drive-thru McDonalds. When she receives no response, Ruby shifts her weight on the hard bench. "I don't like this!"

Still, nothing.

"Right, I don't care if it's a sin Gen. I'm gonna go!" Ruby stands, draws back the curtain, and steps out into a sanctuary that is suddenly very crowded, unprecedentedly crowded—with men and women and children all packed into the pews. Ruby freezes—terrified. She expects someone to notice her, chastise her for being disrespectful, but they're all too caught up in what Father Thomas is saying up at the pulpit.

Was there a second round? She'd thought the confirmation was over. And Gennie. Where's Gennie? Ruby peeks behind the curtain to the priest side of the confessional, but it's empty. Gennie must have snuck out to front hall.

Ruby comes to this conclusion like someone in the midst of a dream. The pieces don't quite fit, but her brain is still trying to make sense of it. And so yes, *of course* Father Thomas is giving another sermon. *Of course* everyone's clothes are different and the church feels different—hot and humid and suffocating when just moments ago it had been cool and airy and quiet.

Ruby feels a sense of relief shiver through her body as she leaves the sanctuary. Were those Gennie's parents up front? She's afraid to go back and look. Instead, she stops to take a deep breath, leaning against a table by the wall. Here, she notices the pamphlets. Dozens of them. All printed on glossy paper. She picks one up to find a school picture of Gennie smiling up at her from the title page, the words *In Memoriam* printed in swirly script beneath it.

Ruby's stomach coils. "Gen?" she says the word like speaking her friend's name will somehow manifest the girl herself. When this proves ineffective, she flips open the pamphlet. It's a recitation of Gennie's accomplishments. Drama Club. Cross Country. Straight A's. Gennie hates Cross Country and gets more B's than A's, but the pamphlet doesn't mention any of these things. *The O'Reilly's were on their way home from a local restaurant after celebrating Genevieve's confirmation when their car was struck and our beautiful Genevieve was taken from us too soon…*

Something in the coiling of Ruby's stomach snaps. She's sure she can hear blood. Taste burning. Is this an aneurysm? It feels like an aneurysm. Her uncle had once survived an aneurysm and said it felt strange, like nothing in him was working the way it was supposed to. Ruby drops the pamphlet, stumbling back towards the sanctuary. Only her legs feel like doll legs that have been put on backwards. Tripping, she opens the doors just in time to see Gennie's mother join Father Thomas at the pulpit. Gennie's little brother, Daniel is nearby, tears streaming down his face.

Wrong. All wrong. Burning. Brain. Aneurysm.

Ruby makes a frantic—desperate—dash to the confessional, leaps inside and swings the velvet curtain closed behind her, collapsing in a pile onto the bench as she starts to heave—big, airless sobs. Her throat burn. *Gennie. Gennie. Gen—*

Someone pulls open the curtain with excessive force. Ruby jumps at least six feet in the air. "Ruby Tuesday?" chirps a sing-songy voice. It's Gennie. Not the Gennie from the school picture, but Gennie with her lavender dress and curly hair. Confirmation Gennie. "What's the matter?"

Ruby feels a scream loosen and dissolve in her mouth. "*Look!*" she scrambles to point out the mourners, but stops when she realizes they aren't any. The sanctuary is empty again. "You…" Ruby stammers. "They…"

Before she can reconsider the possibility that she's having some sort of medical fit, the sanctuary doors open. Ruby flinches, but it is only Daniel—his face glistening not with tears but with cake frosting smeared in the corner of his mouth. "Where have you two been?"

Gennie scowls. "None of your business!"

"Well, Dad says we can go out tonight!" he grins. "A special dinner. Anywhere you want!"

Emily Ruth Verona received her Bachelor of Arts in Creative Writing and Cinema Studies from the State University of New York at Purchase. In 2014 she won the Pinch Literary Award in Fiction. She is a Bram Stoker Award nominee, a Jane Austen Short Story Award Finalist, and a Luke Bitmead Bursary Finalist. Previous publication credits include fiction and poetry featured in several anthologies as well as magazines such as *The Pinch*, *Lamplight Magazine*, *Mystery Tribune*, *Black Telephone Magazine,* and *The Ghastling*. Her essays/articles have appeared online for Tor, Bookbub, Litro, BUST, and Bloody Women. In 2023, she founded the horror book blog *Frightful*. Her novel, *Midnight on Beacon Street*, will be published by Harper Perennial in 2024. She lives in New Jersey with a very small dog.

There's Nothing Quite Like the
MAGPIE MESSENGER
won't you come along?

Curious Corvid
MAGPIE MESSENGER
INDIE PRESS
FESTIVAL LIFE
NEW CONTENT
SNEAK PEEKS INSIDE!
WELCOME HOME

Curious Corvid
MAGPIE MESSENGER
FRUITS OF OUR LABOR
AUTHOR SPOTLIGHTS
PUZZLES & ACTIVITIES
AUTUMN RECIPES
BEHIND THE SCENES
WHAT DO PUBLISHERS WANT?

Curious Corvid
MAGPIE MESSENGER
CIRCUS
POETRY AND PROSE WELCOME
PAID ADVERTISEMENTS AVAILABLE
SUBMISSIONS OPEN OCTOBER 1ST

MAGPIE MESSENGER
RETRO

MESSENGER

Subscription to the
Magpie Messenger
Literary Magazine

AVID READER

A pleasant variety of
material for literature
enthusiasts: the
magazine and eBooks

BOOK CLUB

For literature fans
who crave variety:
the magazine and
the books

$50 monthly

CORVID CRATE

For the literature
super-fans who can't
get enough: all of the
previous tiers and
more.

With multiple subscription tiers
and leveled perks, the Magpie
Messenger has never been more
accessible.

the fool
the fool

One Last Caress

By R. E. Sohl

The first kill had been the hardest.

The girl had given her a good chase, and Pam wasn't quite as young as she used to be. It wasn't just the physical exertion that made it a challenge, she'd never killed anything larger than an insect before. When the girl tripped and fell down into the pine needle strewn white sandy soil she stood over her and hesitated. For a moment she wasn't sure she could actually go through with it. She felt a twinge of pity as the girl looked up at her pleadingly and held her hands out.

It didn't last long. All she had to do to get her resolve back was think about how these people were planning on reopening the camp. The same camp she and her lawyers had worked so hard to shut down. It had only been two years. Two years! She'd say that her poor little Dougie's body was barely cold in his grave if her son had a grave. But his body had never been dredged from the lake and she didn't even have the comfort of a proper memorial to visit. Sure, she had the money from the settlement, but it had never been about the money.

That wasn't the way that she wanted them to pay for all the pain she'd endured. No amount of money could ever give her back what she'd lost.

But their blood, ah, yes their blood - that was another matter! Their blood could bring her boy back to her. All that she needed to do was to gather enough of it. She began chanting the words she'd memorized from the book. The words that would consecrate this killing as a holy sacrifice to the dark powers behind the book. The girl trembled and begged, she ignored it. She could feel a dark power seize hold of her being as she intoned the eldritch incantation. The knife flashed in the sun as it came down over and over, the blood, the sacred blood jetting out, painting Pam in brilliant crimson. The warmth of it was oddly pleasant as it trickled down the corner of her laughing face.

She hadn't expected this to feel so exhilarating, yet that

was the perfect word for it. She hadn't felt this alive since she'd lost her boy. There was such a rush of adrenaline suffusing her being that she found it difficult to stop the stabbing. Yet stop it she must. She had to collect the blood. The precious blood! She couldn't let it all go to waste! The girl had stopped thrashing some time ago. Now Pam pulled out a mason jar from her purse and positioned it so that she could capture some of the blood which was still gushing out. It wasn't that there wasn't enough from this one body alone. Oh no, the problem was that she needed blood from a precise number of victims for the ritual to work, the ritual that would return her boy to her. Thirteen victims to be precise. For thirteen was the sacred number of the dark power whom she now served. She smiled at the irony of it. The thirteenth had also been her son's birthday. It was almost as if it had always been meant to be this way, all of them tangled up in a web of destiny too dense to ever escape from.

She placed the lid back on the jar, wiping the blood from her face as she began the walk back to her jeep. There were more victims to find, unwitting sacrifices to her new master. She knew where to find them.

Fixing up the camp after it had been sitting exposed to the elements for two years was a big job, and there would be plenty of workers for her to prey on. She just had to bide her time, pick them off one by one. Soon, she and Dougie would be reunited and they could be a family again.

She had to act quickly though. The wizard might realize that the book was missing from his library and see what she was up to. It had been foolish for him to let slip that it was a book on the forbidden art of Necromancy he'd forgotten to return to the library of the Inquisition when he'd retired from his secret order of mages, yet he was no fool. He knew what she'd lost and he'd figure out what she was up to sooner or later. He thought he could heal her broken soul by making her his apprentice, by showing her the beauty and magic in the world, but he'd been wrong. She was forever numb to such things now, as dead inside as her son was. There was only one balm for her shattered being, and that was to feel her son in her arms again.

Yes, the other kills had been easy. It became increasingly simpler the more she did it, as more and more of whatever was left of her humanity was

stripped away with each slash of her blade. She could feel her dark lord filling in the gaps where she had been, whispering advice to her, telling her how best to stalk and trap her prey.

She needed the help, she was not a young or a particularly large woman and some of the contractors were quite strong and burly. She'd discovered that the element of surprise was her greatest asset, that and luring them into some of the traps she'd set the night before. One by one they fell, and her mason jar became ever fuller with the blood of her victims. It was difficult to hide the bodies, but somehow she found the strength. It was amazing what one was capable of once you had the proper motivation.

There had been exactly thirteen people working on getting the camp ready to reopen that weekend, precisely the number she needed. She thought once again about the strange web of destiny that she had feared she'd been ensnared in ever since she'd gotten that horrible phone call that her only child, her pride and joy, her beautiful Douglas had drowned in Deercrest Lake. Now she saw that she wasn't trapped in the web at all. She wasn't a victim anymore. She held all the power now. They'd never mock her pain by opening this place again. No other mother would ever have to feel the pain of loss their negligence had visited upon her. She was the spider crouched at the center of the web. It felt good to be the spider. She felt alive again for the first time in two long and terrible years.

She had the whole place to herself now, everyone else was dead. It was time to begin the ritual. If what the book had promised was true, her Dougie would return to her, bigger and stronger and better than ever before. Nobody would ever be able to hurt him ever again. He'd be perfect, immortal.

Pam walked to the edge of the lake, looking out at the black, still waters that had claimed the life of her son. Now it was time to reclaim what had been ripped from her. She took the old book out of her purse, her fingers lingering on the leathery binding, said to be made of human skin. The page she needed was already marked by a bright red cloth bookmark, she flipped it open and began reading.

As she spoke the words aloud, carefully to get the pronunciation just right, a mighty wind stirred up, nearly knocking her down. It was as if all of nature was protesting what she was about to do. She didn't care. She commanded the elements now, the very spirit of the land itself was under her control. She channeled its power to probe beneath the inky depths of the lake, sifting beneath the muck and the mire until she sensed what she was searching for, the remains of her boy.

She poured the blood out of the jar, the pages of the book lapped it up greedily, completely absorbing it, making it a part of itself. Her voice rose in pitch and the wind whipped at her even more violently, sending her hair flying backwards wildly. She urged the angry spirit of the forest to pull Dougie's body from the lake. She watched with ecstasy as his corpse broke the surface, much of the body had been preserved by the mud it had sank down into. Whatever had rotted away she could repair with the magic of the book, with the power of the spirit she now controlled.

The natives had known this spirit, worshipped it as a God. Now she would pour the power of this God into what was left of her son, making him not only whole again, but invincible. She could feel it fighting her and she laughed. The powers behind the book were greater and there was nothing the spirit could do, it was a slave to her will. She forced it inside the cadaver and brought it floating over the surface of the lake towards her. She looked on in triumph as her son's blackened and spoiled flesh began to ripple and bubble, repairing itself. She dropped the book to the ground, her hands outstretched in welcome as her son continued to slowly drift towards her

"No! Pam! Get away from it! That's not your son!" A familiar voice shouted from behind her. She looked over her shoulder and saw the old wizard running towards her. There was someone else with him who she didn't recognize. It didn't matter. They were too late. Nothing could stop her now. She didn't want to hurt her mentor, but she would if he got in her way. She'd stop anyone who tried to interfere with this reunion, it was the one thing she'd dreamed about ever since she'd lost her boy - the chance to hold him again in her arms just one more time, have one last caress.

Her baby was only inches from her now. She smiled for the first time in forever. "That's right, come to mommy."

Now he was here with her again! She could feel his arms wrap around her, so damp, so cold, but also pulsing with *life*!

A new life she had granted to him, one that nobody could ever take away. She looked up at him, his eyes seemed dazed and listless, then suddenly she saw something flickering in them which made her shudder. An unmistakable fury burned behind them. In one brief, terrifying second she finally understood what she'd done. There was nothing left of her son in there, only the spirit she had bound to his decaying flesh - a spirit that was very, very unhappy with her.

Before she could pull away, she felt its teeth tearing into her neck. As she felt her blood squirting out, only to be happily lapped up by the discarded book at her feet, she couldn't help but think with her last thoughts that it had still all been worth it. Just to see him again, to be in his arms one last time. It was all that any loving mother ever could hope for.

Robert Enrico Sohl is the collective consciousness of billions of units of microscopic organic matter. He was born and raised in southern New Jersey, but has resided in Virginia for the last few decades. He is a husband and the father to two rather peculiar offspring. He is the author and illustrator of the Dead End World series of novels chronicling the unusual adventures of Matt Spike, P.I., and his friends. In addition to those tales, he also enjoys writing horror and fantasy short stories.

BANANA PUDDING

Ingredients:

⅔ cup white sugar
⅓ cup all-purpose flour
¼ teaspoon salt
3 eggs, beaten
2 cups milk
2 tablespoons butter, softened
½ teaspoon vanilla extract
2 bananas, peeled and sliced
½ (12 ounce) package vanilla wafer cookies

Directions:

- Combine sugar, flour, and salt together in a medium saucepan. Add eggs and stir well. Stir in milk, and cook over low heat, stirring constantly.
- When the mixture has thickened enough to coat the back of a metal spoon, remove from heat and continue to stir, cooling slightly. Stir in butter and vanilla until smooth.
- Layer pudding with bananas and vanilla wafers in a serving dish. Chill at least 1 hour in the refrigerator before serving.

Be Groovy or leave, man.

Will you stay
or will you go?

HOT COMMODITY

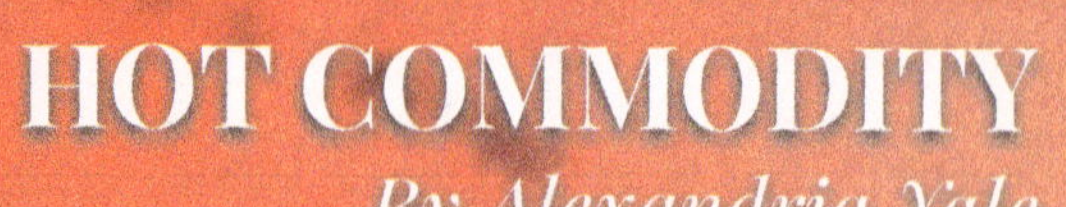

By Alexandria Yale

—

The first sale starts what can't be stopped.

The thrill of profit, biggering possession, opens a world of possibilities—
Chasing after that first, unattainable high.

For more, he will trade what possessions he already has, resources and
assets (the scarcer the better), to only the highest bidder
Dangling the bait just long enough to see desperation

He will trade his time, his knowledge—honest labor for honest wage
But when his own labor is not enough, he will come for yours.

In the past he sacrificed weekends and holidays, friends and family, rest
and relaxation—
He will buy and sell yours as well.

And when that is not enough, he will squeeze harder.

Your health sell for more if you have less time—
So he will buy and sell your time, buying it for less
and selling it for more.

Instead of money, he trades hours from your day
And years off your life.
Sometimes he trades for your future,
In debts he intends you to never finish repaying.

Then he will buy your future, and sell it to children
In exchange for their futures as well.
For he knows as your time becomes scarce,
You will pay him more to compensate.

And when that is not enough, he will come for anything else
you are desperate to keep.

He will come for your passions, your joy, your love
He will come for your childhood and your innocence
All are precious to you; all can be taken
And sold back to you.

When he learns the value of shock,
He will come for common decency, too.

He will come for your faith,
Your privacy,
Your hatred and fear,
Your identity and your safety.

He will sell you politics as though they are your own,
A status symbol product in artificial scarcity,
Pointing to them and causing a scene,
So he can sell you exploitation and slavery
while your back is turned.

He will especially come for your children.
Their vulnerability makes them easy addicts,
And an addict is a good customer.

He will sell deaths. He will sell lives.

And when that is not enough
he will come for your flesh and blood.

And when he has taken you apart,
Cut your bones from their sinews,
Harvested your organs,
Drained your fluids,
Folded and tanned your skin,
Weighed your brain and butchered your muscle,
The Rich Man moves on, drooling blood, wondering:
"What **more** can I sell?"

Join us.
—R

EBON PINION
Curious Corvid
PUBLISHING
Curious Corvid Television

The More You Take AWAY

By Brian Belefant

—————

The time capsule had been buried only five months before, toward the end of the fall session, before the ground got too hard for an eleven-year-old to dig in it. But since then, Robbie had been threatened with death more times than he could count.

Gary Sanchez told Robbie he was going to kill him more than once, most recently when Robbie made the mistake of telling him that his sister Lydia was pretty. She was. Everybody agreed. But Gary hated being told.

And then there was Robbie's sister Holly. She threatened to kill him just about every day, every time he came into her room without knocking or sang too loud or even sometimes when he accidentally looked at her.

Every single one of the Badgers wanted to kill him after that last game because he didn't pass the puck to Mike Loftus, who really wasn't wide open like he said he was, and Robbie took a shot with a minute and 14 seconds remaining in the game and the team down by one. Coach Fuller took them all out for pizza afterward anyway, but nobody would sit next to Robbie or even say anything to him, even after Coach made a speech about how life is not about each goal you make or miss, but about how you play for the whole time.

To be fair, Robbie didn't have a clear picture of what death was. When he woke up one morning to find Roderick floating upside down in the glass bowl he lived in on the dresser, he knew before Mom and Dad said a word that he was dead. But by the time he'd eaten breakfast (and Holly had threatened to kill him for stealing the last pancake––a threat that earned her an unusually stern rebuke that day), Roderick was gone. The next day, Roderick was back. Or maybe it was a new goldfish. Mom called him Roderick, but he looked different, smaller, with a yellowish spot on his side.

At catechism, Mrs. Braithwaite talked about death like it was a good thing. She told the class how glorious it all would be after you died, how you'd be in heaven on the right hand of God, as long as you didn't lie and use swear words. Over the summer she got thinner and thinner, her voice weaker and weaker, until one day in September, Ms. Hilpert started teaching the class and when the kids asked what happened to Mrs. Braithwaite, Ms. Hilpert said how she'd died, gone to heaven and everything, but she said it so sadly that it didn't sound glorious at all.

There was a funeral for Mrs. Braithwaite, but he didn't get to go. Holly did because she was 15 and when he asked her about it, she told him about the hole that was dug in the cemetery, how it was a really neat rectangle and so deep, you couldn't see the bottom.

That's what he was thinking about back in November, when he carried the shovel across the baseball field toward the back of Town Hall the first time, to dig the hole for the time capsule. Robbie got to carry the shovel because he was the fifth grade class president, a position he won fair and square, even after he started telling the other kids not to vote for him after all because Gary wanted to be class president, too, and had cornered Robbie out by the bike racks and told him in no

uncertain terms that he would kill him if he won.

Robbie knew he was going to be dead. That much was certain. It was only a matter of when.

The time capsule was Mr. Braithwaite's idea. He was the social studies teacher and told the kids that a time capsule would be a good way to help them understand that history wasn't just something that happened in the past. He suggested that the class reach out to people who were important to them and ask questions about their lives and what it was like to live in Mapleton. He gave each of the students three photocopies of a form with five questions on it, the idea being that they could ask each of their parents to answer the questions (or in the case of Laura and Lisa Higgens, ask their parents and two other people who they cared about) and then fill out the third one themselves. Most of the kids didn't do the third form. Robbie started, but his hand got tired after writing the answer to the first question, "What do you like best about living in Mapleton?" and he never got around to doing the rest.

When Robbie told Mom and Dad about the time capsule,

Mom said it was beautiful, but Dad wondered if it was just another way for Mr. Braithwaite to get to take a cigarette break on school time. Robbie didn't understand the look Mom shot at Dad over that, but Dad did and said he was sorry.

Like Robbie and Holly and their parents, Mr. and Mrs. Braithwaite went to the ten o'clock mass at Our Lady of Perpetual Sorrow every Sunday, but ever since she died he almost never made it all the way through the sermon. Sometimes, Father Michael didn't even start the sermon before Mr. Braithwaite would excuse his way to the far aisle and make his way out of the main doors, his hand––the hand he always used to hold Mrs. Braithwaite's hand with, whenever the two of them were together––his hand already extracting a cigarette from the pack he kept in his jacket pocket before opening the door as quietly as he could and letting himself out.

Once he was out, Mr. Braithwaite didn't come back. But he didn't go home, either. He stayed out front of the church for the remainder of the service, starting the next cigarette before the embers of the previous one had died. When the congregation filed out, he would stub out his cigarette and join them for small talk and to say hello to Father Michael. You could always tell where he'd been standing because of the halo of cigarette butts on the ground there.

The time capsule was supposed to be a fifth grade project, but word got out and some of the sixth graders wanted to join in. Before long some of the teachers and a lot of the other kids wanted to join, too, and then the Mayor came by the classroom to talk to the kids about what it's like to be the Mayor and when Alicia Garfield asked him to, he said he'd be honored to fill out the form himself.

After the Mayor made his contribution, all sorts of people outside of the school wanted to participate. It seemed like every day, Mr. Braithwaite would give the class an assignment and leave to go make another stack of forms for all the new people who wanted to fill one in. Mr. Murphy, who ran the Dempsy Diner, got every single one of his employees to fill out a form. Even Jared, who worked as a dishwasher and never said a word and everybody thought he was so stupid he didn't even know how to read. Almost all of the doctors and nurses at the Mapleton Hospital filled one out too. And when Father

Michael made it part of his announcement at church a couple of weeks after Mrs. Braithwaite died, just about everybody took a form on the way out of the sanctuary and even more impressive, brought them back the next week, some of them smudged where tears had fallen on the papers where the people were writing. Mr Carlyle donated an extra big box from his office supply store and Ms. Jeffers provided a special shiny shovel from her garden supply store, with a big red bow tied to the handle.

It was the duty of the class president to dig the hole for the time capsule and Robbie fulfilled his obligation with enthusiasm. Even though it was hot for November, he didn't take off the jacket and tie that Mom and Dad made him wear and it was a good thing, too, because the Mapleton Gazette sent a reporter and a photographer to document the ceremony.

Robbie wasn't flustered at all that the whole entire town showed up to watch him dig that hole. Like Mrs. Braithwaite would have said, it wasn't all about him, anyway. The Mayor made a speech, one with a lot of stuff about love in it. For a happy occasion, everybody seemed pretty serious, so Robbie made sure to be serious, too, and made the edges of the hole as straight

as he could, like he was digging a grave.

It fell to the class vice president to make the map so that in 25 years they could find their way back to the time capsule and Gary didn't seem to take that job as seriously as Robbie thought he should. He lost count of the number of steps from the corner of the building to the oak tree, which Gary figured didn't really matter, since the tree wasn't going anywhere. When he said that, Mr. Braithwaite looked like he suddenly had to sneeze—his eyes got watery and he kind of held his breath—but then he said, in a voice that was so gentle it could have been Mrs. Braithwaite talking, "What if the tree is gone in 25 years when it's time to dig up the time capsule?" Gary went back to do the count again.

Mr. Braithwaite's explanation seemed wise, but as Robbie thought about it, he wondered what if the building wasn't there, either?

This time it was different. This time as they headed out of the school yard toward Town Hall it felt like they were fixing a mistake instead of doing something important. Mr. Braithwaite was in the lead again, sucking on a cigarette like it was air itself, the only thing he could breathe in the poisonous atmosphere the rest of them inhabited. Gary trailed behind, not talking to him. Again. Still.

When Robbie told Holly about having to dig up the time capsule, she said, "What gets bigger the more you take away?" The riddle stumped Robbie and he'd like to have asked Mr. Braithwaite to help him out with it, but he could tell Mr. Braithwaite wasn't in a mood to talk riddles.

Unlike back in November, when the entire class paraded over to Town Hall, this time it was only Robbie and Gary and Mr. Braithwaite tromping across the brown grass, brittle with frost, like parchment. Nobody wore anything special, just their parkas and their beanies and their gloves. Gary counted out the steps from the tree toward the light pole and when he got to 148 he stopped. It didn't seem like the right spot to Robbie, but Gary was class vice president, after all, and Robbie didn't feel like he had the authority to question Gary's methods.

Besides, there was one of those digging machines right on top of the spot where Robbie was sure the time capsule actually got buried. Mr. Braithwaite said it was there to repair the

gas line and that was the reason that the time capsule needed to be moved.

Better to have the class take care of it than to leave it to the city, with their big equipment that might mess up the box.

It turned out that Gary had found the right spot after all and it wasn't long before the shovel thudded against the metal of the box.

"Told you that's where it was," Gary snarked at him.

"Yeah, well I dug the hole."

"Yeah, but you didn't want to."

"Doesn't matter. I did."

"You're an idiot."

"You're the idiot."

Mr. Braithwaite took the cigarette away from his lips. "Boys. Cut it out." They did, but not willingly.

Mr. Braithwaite led the boys to a different spot, one closer to the building. He carried the big metal box like it was sleeping, like he didn't want to wake it up, cradling it in his arms. He came to a bit of a rise near some azalea bushes, and looked around as if to appraise

the view from there. "Let's put it here," he said, pointing to a spot where an orange line had been painted on the dead grass.

"What about the map?" Robbie asked.

"We'll make the map backwards, from here to the corner of the building, then turn it around so we can find our way back in 25 years." The answer seemed to satisfy everyone involved, so Mr. Braithwaite put the box gently down and then stepped away to light another cigarette.

"You're such an idiot," Gary remarked, quietly, so Mr. Braithwaite wouldn't hear him.

"No I'm not," Robbie replied.

"Yes you are," Gary said.

"Yeah, well your sister is pretty!"

Gary punched Robbie on the shoulder and even though he was the one holding the shovel, Robbie felt like this might be it. This might be when Gary killed him. Mr. Braithwaite wasn't even looking at them. He was several steps away, cigarette to his lips, staring off at the workers starting up their digging machine.

"Go to hell, Gary!" Robbie said, careful to keep the words quiet so that only Gary and not Mr. Braithwaite or God could hear.

Gary charged him, shoving him off balance. Robbie wanted to shove Gary back, but he'd already committed one transgression and he could feel Mrs. Braithwaite's reproachful look even though she was dead, buried in some other ground on the other side of town. Instead, he attacked the ground with the shovel, slamming it into the hole over and over, flinging the dirt in the general direction of Gary, but not directly at him.

The blade hit something metal. The shock carried up the handle and jarred his hands, making them quiver. Mr. Braithwaite heard the sound, but had no time to say anything before Robbie slammed the shovel into the ground again. This time the clank was followed by an audible hiss, a hiss like the sound that Gary's bike tire made when Robbie poked his pencil into it. But the memory of the bike tire was secondary. Something else. Something else came to him. It was summer. The feeling of summer. After playing outside in the sprinklers for so long that his skin felt tight and red from the sun. And Dad was

over at the grill. That was it, the grill. Dad was starting it up, about to make his famous hamburgers. It was a moment that happened repeatedly, throughout the summer, and it had a distinctive smell. A smell that came from the grill.

The association was so powerful that Robbie froze. He stood, shovel poised to strike another blow, washed over by a moment not now, but either eight months ago or two months into the future, but so present, so powerful. He breathed in deeply to collect as much of the scent as he could.

Mr. Braithwaite's voice came sharp. "Robbie!" Robbie turned, turned in time to see Mr. Braithwaite's face, mouth open, cigarette stuck to his lower lip. A flame stretched upward from the end of a match, reaching for something no longer there, toward an empty spot where the tip of the cigarette had been. The word, his name, still hung in the frosty air, a cloud of breath, slowly dissipating.

And then a flash.

In that instant, his last instant, Robbie figured it out. He knew the answer to the riddle.

©2023 Brian Belefant. Used with permission.

Brian Belefant used to be good looking, but now he has a dog, and not just any dog, but a friendly, goofball dog who loves everybody except Santa Claus.

Brian has won several awards for his writing. Most recently, his short story The Beneficiary was shortlisted for the Backchannels 2023 Fiction Prize. His novella The Sultan of Garbage is scheduled to be published by Atmosphere Press.

He's currently at work on his second novel.

NOW from Libby's...
SLOPPY JOES
with BEEF

Libby's
BARBECUE SAUCE
AND BEEF
FOR
SLOPPY JOES

A zippy mixture of lean ground beef... in a zesty sauce of tomato, beef broth, onion, green pepper and spices. Great on spaghetti, noodles or rice, too!

Libby's

GET IT BY THE CARTFUL
FOR INSTANT ENTERTAINING
AND HANDY-DANDY FAMILY FARE

CLASSIC, HOMESTYLE Sloppy Joes

Ingredients:

1 ½ pounds extra-lean ground beef

½ onion, diced

1 green pepper, diced

2 cloves garlic, minced

2 cups water, divided

¾ cup ketchup

2 tablespoons brown sugar

1 teaspoon Dijon mustard

1 ½ teaspoons salt, or to taste

½ teaspoon ground black pepper

1 dash Worcestershire sauce

1 pinch cayenne pepper, or to taste

Directions:

- Place ground beef and onion in a large skillet over medium heat; cook and stir until beef is browned and crumbled, about 10 minutes.
- Stir in green pepper and garlic; cook and stir until softened, 2 to 3 minutes. Add 1 cup water and stir, scraping the pan to dissolve any brown flavor bits from the bottom of the skillet.
- Stir in ketchup, brown sugar, Dijon mustard, salt, black pepper, and Worcestershire sauce. Add remaining 1 cup water and bring mixture to a boil. Reduce heat to low and simmer, stirring occasionally, until liquid has evaporated and mixture is thick, about 40 minutes.
- Season with salt, black pepper, Worcestershire sauce, and cayenne pepper.
- Enjoy!

Wait...
where are you?
—
Oh no! You wandered too far and ended up in *The Backrooms*.
Escape quickly or you'll be lost forever—
and watch out for Mr. Mandela!

Answers to puzzles in next issue

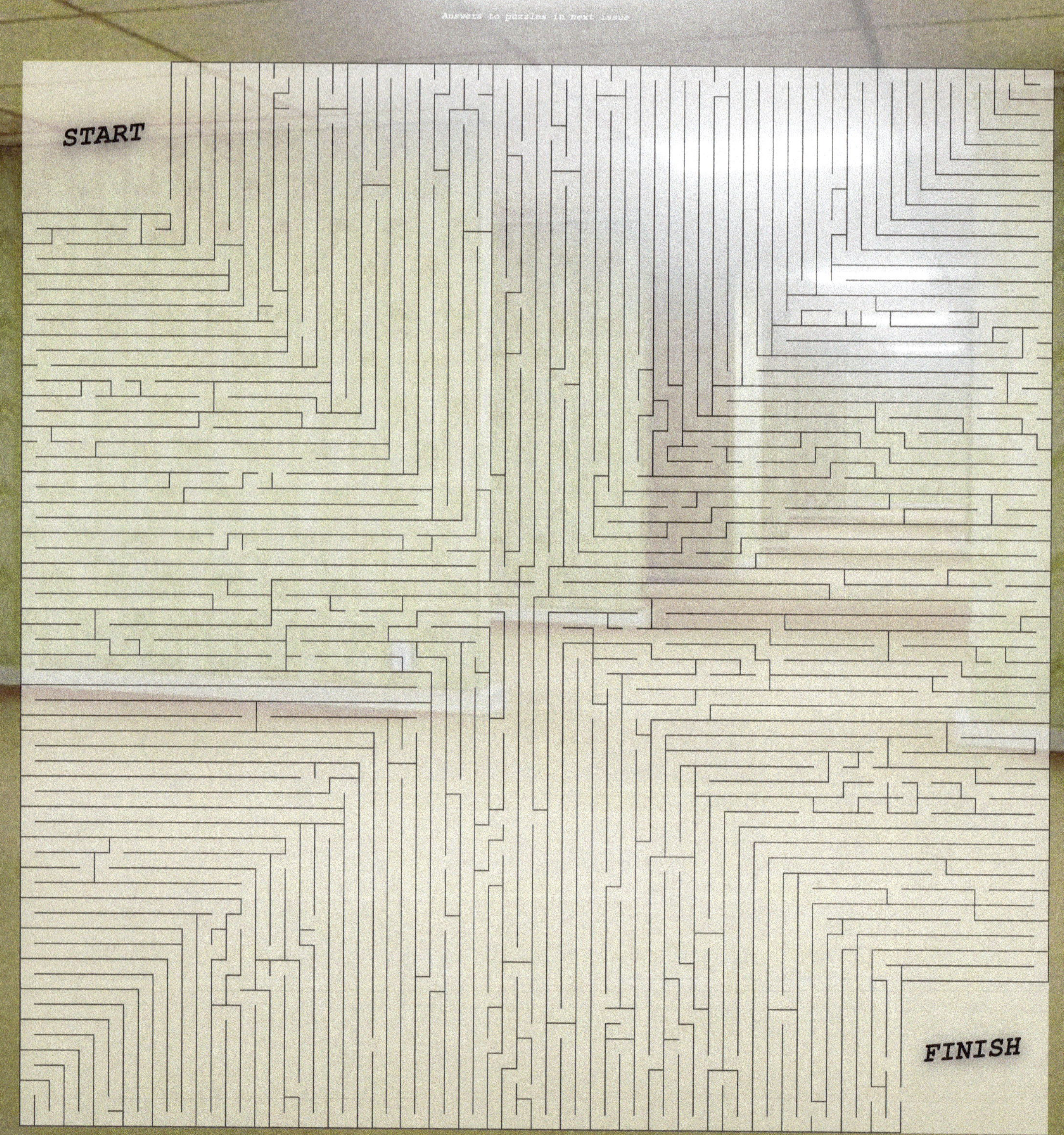

START
FINISH

Pumpkin Jack

By Mark Piggott

Belvidere, NJ – October 31, 1955

Tommy stumbled through the cornfield, desperate to keep his footing on the uneven surface. He could see his breath billow in the frosty night air as he huffed, nearly winded by his fear. He tilted his plastic devil mask back on his head to keep his vision clear as he hurried past the tall stalks of corn. His costume was not very flexible and difficult to run in. The dried corn was ready to be harvested, food for the animals during the cold winter. For now, it provided cover for the terrified ten-year-old.

"We're coming for you, Tommy Lester! You egged the wrong house!" screamed his pursuers. Tommy knew he shouldn't have tempted fate on Halloween. He loved a little mischief and always carried a few eggs to hit the houses of people who were mean to him or his family, but he had a score to settle.

Bobby Forrester broke his sister Penny's heart. He played a trick on her by asking her out to the big Barn Dance. She was so excited that she even went out and bought a new dress for the occasion, but it was all a ruse. Bobby dumped her for another girl, Candy McAllister, a rival of Penny. They did it to "teach her a lesson," or so they said, so Tommy decided to teach them a lesson in return.

Normally, Tommy would egg the house, but tonight, he hit Bobby's house AND his brand-new Thunderbird. The problem was that Bobby was in the backseat of the car with Candy, and they saw him, along with some of his buddies having a party in the house. Tommy ran as fast as he could, taking a shortcut through Willow Brook Farm to get home, but he was a middle schooler being pursued by three high schoolers.

If I can reach the pumpkin patch, I'll be okay. He ran this way home regularly, so Tommy was confident he'd make it, but tonight was different. He had a big bulky flashlight in one hand and his plastic pumpkin filled with his trick-or-treat candy in the other hand. He didn't want to lose either, so he kept a tight grip on both.

"You're dead! Do you hear me, Tommy Lester . . . Dead!" Bobby shouted as he and his friends continued their pursuit of the scared little boy. "And come Monday, I'm going to tell the school that your sister was a whore, that she did it with the whole football team! She'll

never be able to show her face in school again!"

He continued to taunt Tommy, but it only made the little boy angry. Bobby Forrester was the "Big Man on Campus," and he always ensured that you knew it. Besides being a major jerk, he was a top scholar, football team captain, and all-around athlete. No one ever stood up to him until tonight. Tommy knew he had to be the one to teach this bully a lesson.

"Come on, Lester, the longer you make us chase you, the harder the beating you're gonna get," one of Bobby's friends added. Tommy didn't listen to the taunts. He focused on the path ahead.

Once I get past the hedgerow, I'll be in the clear. Tommy could see the stone fencing dividing the two sects of land, separating the cornfield from the pumpkin patch. He was nearly there, gasping for air to make that last push. His legs strained and hurt, but he couldn't stop. His life depended on it.

Tommy exited the cornfield and climbed over the stone hedgerow. A hand grabbed his collar as he threw his leg over the fence, nearly choking him. He dropped his flashlight and trick-or-treat bucket, spilling candy all over the ground. He looked back to see another of Bobby's teammates—Greg Wilson, the

star wide receiver. He was fast on the gridiron, so he must have run ahead to catch Tommy.

He pulled Tommy back across the hedgerow, grabbing him tightly around the arms. His grip was crushing as the skinny ten-year-old struggled against him. "Quit squirming, jackass. You brought this on yourself," Greg said as he tightened his grip, causing Tommy to scream.

"Let go of me, you jerk! You're hurting me!" Tommy shouted as he flailed his legs about. He stopped struggling when he saw Bobby break through the cornrow with his other teammate behind him. Kenny Brockton was Bobby's center on the football field, always there to protect his quarterback. Tonight was no exception for this behemoth farm boy.

Bobby took a couple of deep breaths. He was angry, really pissed off that this kid made him run through a cornfield. He didn't say a word. He took out a comb from his pocket and ran it through his perfect blonde hair, straightening it after his long run. Bobby adjusted his letterman jacket, grinning wickedly as he stepped up to his prey.

"Let me go, Bobby Forrester, or you'll regret it!" Tommy demanded, but that only made the three high schoolers laugh. Bobby, however, wasn't laughing when he smacked Tommy across the face.

"The only one that's gonna regret it is you and your ugly ass sister," Bobby said. "I'm going to make sure of that. She'll get hers later, but now it's your turn."

"Do you want to take him back to the house and deal with him there, Bobby? Candy will want to get some licks in," Greg reminded him.

"No, I'll let her take care of his sister," Bobby said. "I'm going to teach this punk a lesson tonight." He looked around and saw something off in the distance. In the middle of the pumpkin patch was a scarecrow, standing alone. It was strapped to a stake with a jack o' lantern for a head. Seeing the scarecrow gave Bobby a great idea.

"Let's go, bring him over here," Bobby said, jumping over the stone hedgerow. Greg handed Tommy over while he and Kenny climbed over after them. The three dragged him through the pumpkin patch, fighting back along the way until they reached the scarecrow.

It was a lanky straw man wearing a ragged dark suit stuffed with hay and a flowing red scarf dancing in the cool autumn breeze. Its head was a jack o' lantern, with a jagged grin smiling at you no matter which direction you looked at it from. It terrified crows and whoever might come across it.

"Pull that thing down from there, Kenny," Bobby ordered, but the big lineman kept his distance.

"No way, I ain't touching that thing," Kenny said as he backed away. "You do it, Greggy."

"Chicken shit," Greg remarked as he passed Tommy over Kenny while he pulled the scarecrow down from his perch, tossing it aside like garbage. Bobby took some of the rope that secured the effigy on the pole and tied the scared little boy to it. He tightened it securely around his wrists, ensuring he couldn't escape.

Before he backed up, Bobby punched him across the face. Tommy spit blood and a tooth, bleeding profusely from his mouth, but he did not cry—he did not scream—and that pissed off the star athlete. He punched him repeatedly, swelling and bloodying his eye and cheek from the abuse.

"Take it easy, Bobby. He's just a kid," Greg said. "Do you want the cops pinning an assault charge on you?" Bobby knew the police wouldn't touch him, not with the state championship on the line, but he had to admit, Greg was right. If he kept this up, he could severely injure or kill the kid. Bobby leaned down to be at eye level with his captive, pulling his hair so Tommy would look at him.

"You listen to me, Tommy Lester, and listen good. You can spend the night out here and think about that little prank you pulled on me. In the morning, we'll come out and set you free. You tell your parents or the cops about any of this, and I will make your sister's life Hell for the rest of the school year. They won't believe a little troublemaker like you anyway. So be smart and take your punishment."

Tommy didn't answer him. He didn't say anything at all. Bobby let his hair go, but not before getting in one last lick by slamming his head into the post. The three laughed it off as they turned to leave.

"Pumpkin Jack . . ." Tommy finally said in a soft murmur, getting the three high schoolers' curious attention.

"What did you say, runt?" Greg asked. Tommy raised his head and stared at them, looking through one bloodshot eye as he spoke with a slight lisp due to his missing tooth.

"Beware the stare of Pumpkin Jack!

"Pumpkin Jack will take you back,

"Back beyond the grave.

"It's such a fright on Halloween night,

"Under a bitter harvest moonlight,

"Where only fools will brave."

The three teenagers laughed at the poem he recited and the change in his voice from the beating. "Is that supposed to frighten us?" Bobby wondered. "Some old wives tale our parents told us to make sure we didn't wander around late on Halloween?"

"It's not a story. It's true," Tommy interrupted. "Why do you think I was trying to get to the pumpkin patch? I knew I'd be safe once I crossed the stone hedge. You were just stupid enough to bring me here."

The three boys continued to laugh at Tommy. "Damn, Bobby, I think you hit his head one too many times," Kenny joked. "I think you knocked a screw loose." They laughed even louder, but Tommy didn't. He smiled wickedly, showing off his missing tooth, quickly quieting the football players.

"You don't get it, do you?" Tommy crowed. "You shouldn't have taken him down from his perch and disturbed his Halloween. This is all your fault."

The bright moonlight kept everything well-lit in the open field, but a shadow suddenly fell across the boys. A scraping sound emanated from behind the trio, like stepping on a creaky floorboard. They turned around slowly and looked up at a horror growing behind them.

It stood nearly ten feet tall, a gangly creature of enormous size that towered over them. Stick fingers stretched out like skeletal hands reaching from the grave. Its pumpkin head glowed in an unnatural light as flames flickered like a Halloween jack o' lantern. The smile wasn't carved in the gourd; instead, it moved like a living creature. Pumpkin Jack was alive and tending to its pumpkin patch. Some weeds needed to be pulled.

Tommy laughed as he watched the three teenagers panic—Greg tried to take off while Kenny froze there in fear. On the other hand, Bobby scrambled to hide from the monster behind his captive. He watched in horror as the scarecrow grabbed Greg by the collar, stepping on Kenny and holding him down. For an awkward-looking demon, its strength was incredible.

Pumpkin Jack roared a howl, chilling them to the core, especially Bobby, as he trembled behind Tommy. The little boy could only laugh at their precarious predicament. "Make

him stop! Make him stop!" Bobby screamed, shaking Tommy vigorously. "I'm sorry, we'll let you go! Just make him stop!"

"It's too late for you, Bobby Forrester, too late for all of you," Tommy said. "You'll never hurt anyone ever again, but on the other hand, you'll be hurting forever!"

Bobby didn't know what he meant by that until he looked up and saw the face of Pumpkin Jack inches from his. The flames burning inside his pumpkin head glowed bright but burned cold, sending shivers through his soul. Jack grabbed him by the face and laughed, silencing his screams before the beast looked down at Tommy. There was no fear in the eyes of the trick-or-treater as he smiled at Jack.

"Thank you for saving me, Jack. You always take care of me." Jack nodded his pumpkin head while tightening his grip on Bobby's face. There would be no peace for these three interlopers. They belonged to Pumpkin Jack.

Belvidere, NJ – November 1, 1955

A police car pulled up outside the Lester home, followed by three other vehicles. Sheriff Bill Watson stepped out of his car

while the parents of the three football players jumped out of their vehicles. The odd passenger getting out of one car was a pretty blonde teenager wearing a poodle skirt and a tight angora sweater hugging her ample breasts.

Candy McAllister was more angry than worried. Bobby, Greg, and Kenny took off after little Tommy Lester after he egged the house and car. When they never came home, everyone started to worry. Sheriff Watson tried to calm the antsy parents down and forced Candy to hang back with them while he tended to the problem.

He knocked on the door and waited patiently until Tommy's mother opened it. She looked out at the ensembled group on her front lawn and knew instantly what this was about. "Sorry to bother you, Mrs. Lester, but three high school students are missing. They were last seen chasing your boy Tommy after he 'egged' the Forrester house."

"Oh, I know all about it, sheriff. Tommy, come here!" she shouted until her son walked up to the door, still wearing his Halloween costume, his face bruised and eye still bloodshot from the beating he received. "Look at what Bobby Forrester did to my son! That maniac beat my son and left him tied up in the pumpkin patch on Willow Brook Farm. It's a good thing Tommy got free and made it home. I was about to call you, Sheriff Watson, to file a complaint against those three hooligans for what they did to my boy."

"My son is no criminal! That's your little bastard!" Bobby's dad shot back before the sheriff snapped his finger at him to quiet down. He took the hint and backed down, but Candy didn't as she stormed toward them.

"Don't lie, Tommy Lester! Do you know what happened to Bobby? I know you do, you little shit!" she screamed as the sheriff had to restrain her. Tommy wanted to smile, but he kept his cool and looked solemnly at the people, holding tightly onto his mother's hand.

"I don't know what happened to them," Tommy said with cold confidence. "After they beat me and left me to spend the cold night in the middle of the pumpkin patch, I got my hands free and came straight home. If you don't believe me, go to the pumpkin patch near the scarecrow in the middle of the field. That's where they left me."

The sheriff nodded, wanting to diffuse the situation as quickly as possible. He shooed everyone back to the cars, urging them to follow him to Willow Brook farm to investigate Tommy's story further. Reluctantly, they all agreed to his request, including a subtle shove pushing Candy toward the car.

They waited at the door until they left before Tommy's mother closed the door and pulled her son inside. She didn't see the evil grin on Tommy's injured face. The little boy knew the truth.

When they reached the pumpkin patch and made their way to the scarecrow, all they would find was the rope coiled on the ground. It would prove Tommy's story that he was tied up, but there would be no sign of the three teenagers. It was as if they had disappeared off the face of the Earth.

All they would find sitting at the foot of the scarecrow were three pumpkins, seemingly carved with faces in pain, torment, and agony. The troublemakers waited to be smashed by kids or pulped into slop for the pigs. This was the fate of those who crossed paths with Pumpkin Jack, suffering a life worse than death as they lingered to their last.

©2023 Mark Piggott. Used with permission.

Remembering Impetigo's *"Horror of the Zombies"*

By Michael Perret

RESTRICTED R — STRONG ADULT LANGUAGE OFFENSIVE CONTENT THROUGHOUT — Under 17 Requires Accompanying Parent or Adult Guardian ®

It's 1992. I'm 14. My friend Shawn is already in high school. Maybe he's 16. A few months ago he shared a compilation cassette with me of heavy ▓▓▓▓▓p shi▓▓▓got from one of those miraculous oases of a small town record store. It was run by a radical old punk hippie couple (maybe, I was too inexperienced to note the traces left by their various scenes) in Conroe, TX. I went into their record store once and saw they had a Christmas card from Gwar (dating back to Hell-o by my assessment) and wanted to buy that, but they laughed and declined. NOT FOR SALE. They were cool as fuck.

▓▓▓▓ In those days I would visit my older cousin over the winter and summer breaks and had gotten to know some of her high school friends. Shawn was one of those. My cousin was into Madonna, Shawn was into Slayer.

On that compilation album Shawn specifically pointed out one song with raised eyebrow and a knowing get-the-▓▓▓-ready look, this-is-going-to-blow-your-▓▓▓ng-mind. I got it. It did. "Revenge of the Scabby Man" by Impetigo. Distorted bass intro, insane death-to-spasz vocals, Peter Lorre-sounding deep cut sample intro ("The wound is now being infected with gangrene pus...") Shawn didn't know about my profoundly sensual affection for Peter Lorre, probably dating back to a childhood watching 20,000 Leagues Under the Sea. Frankly I didn't either, not consciously, but this song spoke to me. It screamed, I AM THE HEAVIEST ▓▓▓▓ YOU'VE HEARD TO DATE, AND WHAT YOU WANT IS THE HEAVIEST!

I tracked down the record that cut came off of. Ultimo Mondo Cannibal (1990). The cover art was of some indigenous people carving up a white body. I didn't need to know this at the time, but it was referencing the brutal 70s cult horror classic Cannibal Holocaust about a film crew that plunges into the Amazon to film a documentary about the indigenous people living there only to get eaten by cannibals. Back home in Italy, the filmmaker was prosecuted on suspicious of actually murdering one of the indigenous actors (she gets impaled in the movie) and had to demonstrate how the scene was filmed without actually murdering anyone. Perhaps the endpoint, the most extreme stage of popular music, that music produced by a few kids who start a band and get to rocking in one of their parent's garages, is the subgenre that usually goes by the name goregrind. Credited to the Liverpool band Carcass, who effectively invented it with their first record Reek of Putrefaction (1988), goregrind is characterized by down-tuned screams, superfast drumming (blast beats), very short songs, song titles like "Vomited ▒▒▒▒ Tract" and extremely graphic cover art. The cover of Reek of Putrefaction consists of a collage of images cut out from one of the band member's sister's pathological anatomy textbooks. She was in nursing school, or so the story goes. With some of the members in the band being vegetarian, an anti-animal cruelty (and anti-human) ethos got associated with the genre, most notably with bands like Cattle Decapitation, while other bands took the dead human body cover art to new extremes and established a brutal memento mori branch of goregrind (Last Days of Humanity). Another tradition was established almost immediately by Impetigo: extreme gore, deep-cut-horror-film-sample goregrind (for lack of a better name)! And that was Ultimo Mondo Cannibal, and that was

my introduction to the heaviest of the heavy. This was a cassette I definitely needed to keep out of sight, even as Impetigo became my favorite band I never got to talk about.

In those days, the early 90s, aside from local record stores (I bought Ultimo at that bad record store in Conroe), underground music got distributed nationally through catalogues. I don't remember how I got signed up for the crazy ▒▒▒ catalogue I would get, but it was in one of those that I learned that Impetigo had a new record out. This was a holy ▒▒▒ moment, and I immediately got my mother's checkbook and wrote them a letter ordering the new album (everything was released on cassette in those days) and a t-shirt. I remember putting my heart into that letter, but I don't remember a word of what I wrote. When the package arrived, another one of my cousins was spending the night. William was a year or two younger than me. He'd started visiting Conroe with me over the breaks and was friends with Shawn now too. We both were into horror movies. Speaking of horror movies, Impetigo had pushed me beyond Nightmare on Elm Street. Nazi zombies, ▒▒▒▒▒▒▒▒ streetcleaners, things I can't stomach now, but somehow then... While I was mesmerized by the cassette, Horror of the Zombies (1992), William pulled out the t-shirt and cried out, "Exorcism Be

████!" The front of the shirt had a drawing of naked woman being approached by some zombies in a cemetery, but the back of the shirt had some pentagrams and the phrase William had excitedly blurted out. I somehow thought that would be the sticking point for my church-going mother, not the cartoonishly misogynistic threat on the front (which would be the obvious sticking point for me today). There was also a cheaply printed flyer advertising Impetigo on one side with some evil gore, and a (probably) ████ grind band on the reverse with photos of naked woman, vulvas all hastily sharpied out. I recall mentioning my age in my fan letter. I promptly gave William the shirt. He had no problem wearing whatever he wanted.

Horror of the Zombies (1992) became the first work of art that I felt to be a true masterpiece. I still rave about it, and it's no less awkward today, maybe even more so when happy, polite, normal people unexpectedly meet with my recommendation of a horrific compilation so far from what counts as music to them. And yet, this record was a departure from the goregrind Impetigo had only just developed with their last record into the deep-cut horror movie direction. One of the basic characteristics of goregrind, and grindcore, and extreme hardcore for that matter, is short songs.

Songs under a minute. Twenty-minute full albums with twenty-two songs. Five-minute EPs with 9 songs. Guitar solos...what? With Horror of the Zombies, Impetigo took the horror culture they'd developed in Ultimo Mondo Cannibal and the instruments that begun to master, and created some sick, stomping (slowed down, no blast beats) metal songs, that, though still gurgling, growling and screaming with early Carcass, achieved their own new genre-defining pinnacle.

Some of the films sampled: Wizard of Gore (1970) ("WHAT is real?"), Andy Warhol's Flesh for Frankenstein (1973) (Udo Kier explaining, "To know death, Otto, you have to ████ life...in the gallbladder!"), and Let Sleeping Corpses Lie (1974), a film which opens with nude streakers protesting environmental devastation before developing a plot where an experimental radiation-based pesticide sets off some zombie drama. The last song on the album, "Breakfast at the Manchester Morgue", has always been my favorite. It begins by sampling an entire scene from Let Sleeping Corpses Lie followed by a pounding song from the perspective of a horde of zombies waking up at the Manchester morgue. The film ends with the last dead bodies being taken to the morgue, but the viewer knows that one of them is a zombie... Impetigo provided the sequel twenty years later in song form. I can't tell you how ██████ cool this is to me. I mean, the purpose of this essay to try to!

Though Impetigo are not the worst offenders, and Carcass are actually clear of suspicion, the metal scene has always been remarkably misogynistic. In 2016, Jill Mikkelson called it out in an article for Noisey entitled, "It's Time to Stop Making Excuses for Extreme Metal's Violent Misogynist Fantasies." But the "fantasies" or insanely violent lyrics are just a part of it, the behavior sucks too. "I feel pretty safe saying you'd be hard-pressed to find a woman who hasn't encountered some sort of sexist behavior whilst participating in the ██████ forest that is extreme metal." Sara Taylor's dispiriting novel Boring Girls (2015), about a couple girls who get into extreme metal only to find themselves wandering through that "██████ forest", depicts the scene with convincing emotional reality. Sara Taylor is the lead singer The Birthday Massacre, so she would know. It's probably a right of passage for a certain number of young well-intentioned male metal heads to embarrassingly get challenged by a really existing girl on the disgusting, indefensibly preposterous lyrics of a Cannibal Corpse or whoever. In Boring Girls those males get a little more challenged than that.

I don't recall Shawn and I reconvening on Impetigo. They entered my private place. I recall Shawn trying to get me to record the vocals for a cover of "Personal Jesus", a song I'd never heard by a band I'd never heard of. (Lack of taste and education since corrected!) We did spend a glorious evening in his garage with my bass, his guitar and a drum machine looping at 13 beats a second recording a gorenoise demo. It was around some holiday, maybe Thanksgiving, and I had a raspberry seed stuck in my tooth. He said scream about that. We called the project Black Rot. I'd first suggested Black Rot Gism, but he didn't like it, and I guess I lacked the courage of my goregrind convictions.

Not long after that other influences in my life lead me to the fine arts, classical music, poetry and philosophy, and I threw up a wall between my early teenage and my late teenage self. The extremity of my youthful aesthetics had struck me as isolating. Now I feel lucky that at a young age goregrind made its grooves in my cerebellum. Not everybody gets to appreciate what it has to offer. It just sounds like noise, scary noise to them.

Michael Perret

is a poet and translator from Austin, Texas. His translation of the short novel Octavia, the Quadroon was published was published in 2021 by Éditions Tintamarre. His hybrid story "Monsieur Faustin's Gris-Gris" can be found in the Dark New Orleans anthology published by Dark Stroke Books in 2022. His newest collection, The Chimera was published by Curious Corvid Publishing in March of 2023.

AFC
OFF
ON
STEREO
TUNER
TUNER INPUT
0
1
2
3
4
5
STEREO
FM
8
AM
530
TUNER
PHONO
MONITOR
MODE
HI-FILTER
SOURCE
TAPE
STEREO
MONO
OFF
ON
FUNCTION

92 96 100 104 108 MHz
700 800 1000 1200 1400 1600 kHz
NESS
BASS
TREBLE
BALANCE

Topaz Nostalgia

Ravven White

And once upon a time

in the hot summer weather

that singed the freshly poured black tar,

Rick rolling in the background

wafting from the lazy screen door,

she smiled.

Topaz burgundy eyes drifted across pages

of a well-worn book

yellowed; singed from oils

of sweaty hands greedily

turning pages.

Above, the sun passed and faded.

Behind, Rick was silenced

and replaced

by the gentle chirps of midnight peepers

and the fluttering hum of beetle wings.

And she, still snug

in the comforting boughs

of a bendy pine tree that hadn't

grown quite right,

smiled.

I hold her in my memory, ever so gently
in the way she always ought to be.
This is how I should always
like to remember
the girl with topaz burgundy eyes...
Yellowing books out of love,
lost in daydreams of
a make-believe paradise.
Lazy summer days
when she was a child,
truly,
unaware of the stories
she would someday live to write.
©2022 Raven White. Used with permission.

The Original Goths

By Rythian Black

Long I long to see. To see.

The original goth scene.

See the age of gothic art,

Brought to life by spooky hearts.

Meet my idols in my age,

Dance with them the light away.

Long have I longed to listen.

The Banshee's first screams written.

Here the first poetic words,

Of my Idol and The Cure.

The lament of Bella dead.

Read by The Bauhaus Undead.

Long I have longingly felt,

Taste the sadness that was dealt.

The flashing lights of the club.

The fire in those goth's blood.

Against the world like black crows,

I long to join their murder of woes.

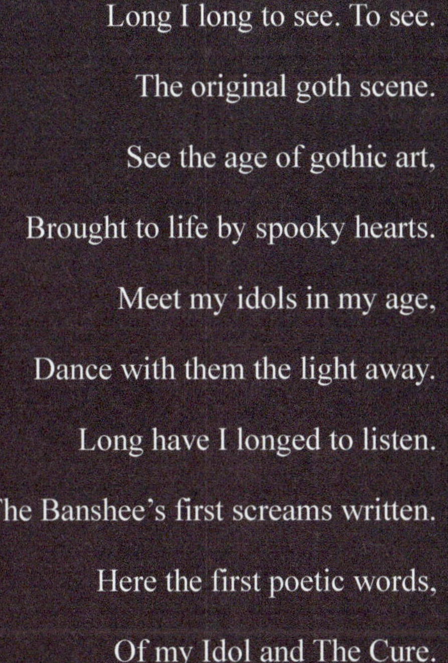

An old soul trapped within the modern realm. Rythian Black seeks to find the magic within the world. A gothic artist with love of the spooky and macabre. Sharing to the world the darker aspects of life and a fondness for the poetic works.

Wonderful way to enjoy Nature's most refreshing flavor
PINEAPPLE UPSIDE DOWN CAKE
So easy to make with....
....Canned Pineapple
Just take a can of crushed Pineapple / or... Pineapple tidbits or chunks...or sliced Pineapple, and follow your favorite upside-down cake method
PINEAPPLE JUICE
CANNED
TROPIC-FRESH
IS WONDERFUL
ANY TIME !

PINEAPPLE UPSIDE-DOWN CAKE

Ingredients:

½ cup butter

1 cup packed light brown sugar

1 (20 ounce) can sliced pineapple

10 maraschino cherries, halved

1 cup sifted cake flour

1 teaspoon baking powder

¼ teaspoon salt

4 large eggs

1 cup white sugar

1 tablespoon butter, melted

Directions:

- Preheat the oven to 325°F (165°C).

- Melt ½ cup butter over very low heat in a 10-inch heavy skillet with a heat-resistant handle or a cast iron pan. Remove from heat; sprinkle brown sugar evenly into the skillet. Arrange pineapple slices to cover the bottom of the skillet. Distribute cherries around pineapples; set aside.

- Sift together flour, baking powder, and salt in a bowl; set aside.

- Separate eggs; place whites in a large mixing bowl and yolks in a smaller bowl.

- Beat egg whites on medium speed until soft peaks form. Add white sugar gradually, beating well after each addition. Beat until medium-stiff peaks form.

- Beat egg yolks at high speed until very thick and yellow. Using a wire whisk or rubber scraper, gently fold egg yolks and flour mixture into whites with an over-and-under motion until blended.

- Fold 1 tablespoon melted butter and almond extract into batter, then spread batter evenly over pineapple in the skillet.

- Bake in the preheated oven until a toothpick inserted in the center comes out clean, 30 to 35 minutes. Loosen cake edges with a table knife. Cool cake for 5 minutes before inverting it onto a serving plate.

Life is not what I expected life to be like. I was a variable or a person who lived outside the system of life. I lived on an edge that few people believe. Do an internet search on Clinton R. Siegle or type in the name on LinkedIn. A wild tale of a Montanan traveling the United States ending up in Bolivia. Where Sundance died, along with years later, Che. Sort of example of legends to live or die up to. The current setting for me. La Paz Bolivia, a cafe close to the embassy. I am watching people. Why? Read far into this tale to find out. The excitement of seeing the day walked by. I got up and followed. I wanted to see where these strangers went. Why? Again, farther into this story, I will explain. The person I followed ducked into a construction site. I had not noticed it there before. At what time did it change or not built or what happened to the home that was there? That question happened a lot these days. My first journals were all about the details changing. Details? Brands, history, people's names, locations, and colors. Everything is changing. Say what? Let me begin with where I remember living for 45 years. According to a poem by me which is censored here. I wrote a poem detailing life on earth. Where? When I searched the Internet, the results showed that earth was on the Sagittarius outer arm of a galaxy 377,000 in diameters. No known black holes. The year 2016 plus or minus and time reference point 4.5 billion years into a future that no longer exists. Why 4.5 billion years? My poem I wrote about how weird life was about to get. Earth was about to step outside

the galaxy for a bit. That bit correlated with 1500 year destruction cycles. (Siegle, 2018, plus or minus billions of years or just the last moment.) One reads about history. Say what? The last time earth stepped outside its galaxy borders. There was a drought so bad in 400 to 600 AD that half of China ate the other half. People forget those tales. If one is a religious person.

The other time, Planet X visited earth. Another drought was noted in the Bible and the Torah when Joseph saved Egypt. Where Egypt gained enough gold to still make it one of the largest gold deposit holders in this time, too. The other notable time? Noah's flood. Again Torah and Bible statement when North America Yellowstone blew. When North America attacked Russia. The water coming from the heat of beaver dams wiped out the valley of the Mediterranean. Where life was easy and good. The visiting red dwarf star along with Planet X was close. Anyway, back to 4.5 billion years. There I wrote that earth math showed earth would run into the next galaxy in 365,000 years. (Siegle) While here? 4.5 billion years. So this is a time traveler journal. Let me make this clear. The mystery is why and how and well. A tale to read while wandering in the night streets. A reason you look at the strangers seated in cafes trying to figure out who or what is going on?

So time travelers journal? Why are you writing it this way? I suppose the last 10 journals I wrote did not meet with anyone's expectations? I mean, what is at stake in a journal, a tale, a mystery

of time, after all? Time? How can you say you are 4.5 billion years old? I have been reading your journal "A wandering mind through the multiverse" since 2017 and well. It is noteworthy. What are you trying to say? I suppose I watch the time of tribulation with speculation. Speculation? Time of Tribulation? Where? Why? That is the end of the story. I am at the beginning. Let me begin with where I was at.

On May 18, 2016, plus or minus 4.5 billion years into a future, I lived on a parallel earth. I wrote poetry. Short pirate stories read by many people at one time. There I can say I read on www.deagel.com that the earth had 8.5 billion people. The United States has 365 million citizens and 29 million illegals. Say what? Are you trying to say you have seen the rapture? Yes, another and no.

The alternative world I awoke on May 19, 2016, was so close to mine. If I had not been vision impaired, I would have not noticed the dramatic change in colors in my room. Quality has changed. It was a better world than mine. In what ways? At first I did not realize the dramatic loss in population. Which was 2.5 billion people? Say what? When I looked I was on an earth with 6 billion people. What I noticed was that the colors were more real. Like stepping from an old color television into a modern color TV. That first day I noticed all the public transportation was much newer. My world we were using late 1990 vans and cars. In this reality? Everything was close to 2013 or newer. Much to my surprise. Where did all this extra money come from? Meaning the improvement was dramatic. I investigated. I did a lot of research from the Internet to books.

What I discovered was a change in empathy and how life went in those different worlds. Meaning? My world in 1967 Roe versus Wade occurred. From that date on to 2016. I knew from radio and political ads that 40 million people had gone because of abortion in my United States. Here is the reality today: Roe versus Wade occurred in 1973.

Since that date, the United States has aborted double the United States citizens. What am I saying? That the rapture is man made via policy changes made to ensure certain populations. Come now, the Bible is not the government. No. But time travel and stories seem to be the truth. The rapture was invented by Darby in the 1840s. Why or how? I speculate on that. I had found 40 million US citizens. In that these realities abort double the babies than in my reality. Still, that does not explain billions or billions. No. Yet, when I searched. I found China actually enforces the one child policy and forces abortions since 1973. So this story is about time travel, rapture, and?

My journal is about my reaction to how life changed. Along with how I have changed since discovering these realities. I worried I was missing people; you see. My Facebook network seemed to be f with profiles that were no longer used. Were they aborted? Did they not survive whatever brought me to this reality in time? If this is not an odd enough question. Think how people that knew me must have felt when I wrote them about these ideas and changes.

My journal recorded how the earth's geographical land masses moved. South America moved for 80 some days going east south. Meaning from where South America

America in my memory for 45 years was. To which is where South America is now below North America, plus 2400 miles east south of that location. Meaning? Santiago, Chile, I was to book a flight there to San Francisco; changed, it was an 11 hour flight. Now? 25 or 27 hours depending on the airline. That is only your memory playing tricks on you. Sure, sure. What about Japan being off the coast of China, not Korea? Or New Zealand, one island above, not below Australia? Or that Mongolia never was part of China? I could go on. I do in some journals for some 100s of examples of changes of things, locations, and realities of things.

So the reality? At first I thought I was in parallel realities. I was on the Sagittarius arm for 80 or more days. Then that changed; too. I went to Pegasus after a while. Now. I suppose I should say that on earth. Wild. Why? The luck there I saw was beyond crazy. I wrote long examples of kids kicking soccer balls into the same two foot area 11 times in a roll. The speed was faster, meaning the bus reaching locations that took 20 minutes in half the time. From there, I noted the earth went to the Orion arm, then the Orion spur, and now the Orion nebula column. To be billions of years old, watching planetary loops each night of a story for you to read the rest. Well. I can point out I am partially blind, one footed, and was a noted poet at one time. So let me say this journal is to investigate for me along the way what has happened to my journals online in every way. From journals. That were online poetry sites, social platforms, and hard hand-written copies. The hard choices I have had to make.

Along with what is my goal in this journal? To change your mind. To change humanity's ending, I suppose. What will happen? For those Ray Bradbury fans, this is where the story gets good. For those that have read this far? Meah. Keep in the journal and get better. For those forced to read this because of some time traveling study course.

Thanks for reading this short story, I suppose. Come along with me for a tale of no return at looking at the surrounding reality in any normal sense of the way. The same way.

What are the dangers of this thought or ideology? My doppelgänger wife sent me to 15 or 17 doctors after I told her what I was seeing. You might pray to God. That magical portals exist and if you are not willing to go. Sometimes you might end up pushed into a new reality.

This journal is to give hope to those people, fearing the Mandela Effect. To realize that they are not alone. That the television Lost had more meaning than one would expect.

This journal is to investigate what I have learned over the years. To think about reality and the significance of what I am trying to communicate.

The obvious issues? I am a partially blind, one-footed insane guy living in La Paz, Bolivia. This complete book might be fiction or nonfiction to him. Reality might change? Your concept of a story might improve something today. While destroying an ideology tomorrow? Investigate a journal entry from the beginning of this journal. Which is no longer available online?

Hard copy.

Last of the ten general reports. Enclosure details of plan longevity according to the Internet. Earth 6.5 billion old from Talon, 123 last of the legion.

Classified Supreme Generals Claw Expeditionary Force Officer Messenger Staff, G-7

16 June 2016 earth date6.5 billion years old Expeditionary Force number 123.

Subject: Plans of German timeline discovered on the internet. Source: Link now defunct recollection information the time wars went badly. Agent Talon 123. This agent is reliable and has worked in the past three operations. On projects to avoid Heaven. He was in close contact with General Slevin, General Miller, and General Flashman. During the following three campaigns. They celebrated his performance for 365 years prior to the Reich's fall on Alimania.

1. A principal messenger sent into the future to detect the breakdown of the system of things. Event has occurred. What exactly? Prior to the astounding rediscovery of Talon 123. Memory contact with program code name Alice. Detail meetings occurred Oct 24 through November 7. At which point they forced Talon 123 to give up the project's end game.

2. Talon 123 states: That all efforts need to fall back to the grid provided via General Slevin. In prior reality reports. Below, the known time has to be done to save them. They leave what little of this reality is in time.

3. Blow reality to be watched by Talon 123. End game scenario to be played out 123 has already lost in the past. This game has no benefit in time. Talon 123 recommends pull out of those able to leave immediately. The end of this timeline is approaching.

Remember, I am writing this journal. To show my investigation of my time travelers through the universe.

What are the final ideological questions to question before I continue? Besides telling you that the rapture is man made, along with government policies? That is your concept of your world.

Specifically, the plural world's system of things needs to change for humanity to survive.

Or? Humanity dies.

That seems like a lot of work for a fiction or nonfiction book to cover. So let me begin again. Starting with what I have discovered. This along with my time as a pushed time traveler into the reality in which I find myself today.

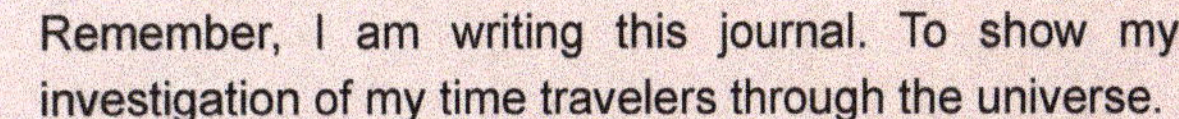

In Retrospect,

90
IEC II/TYPE II HIGH POSITION
SUPER AVILYN CASSETTE SUPER HIGH RESOLUTION
B:
SUPER PRECISION ANTI-RESONANCE CASSETTE MECHANISM
Share your piece on social media
and tag us for a showcase!

Ingredients:

2 refrigerated 9 inch pie crusts, at room temperature, divided

1 tablespoon olive oil, or as needed

2 boneless, skinless chicken breasts, pounded thin

2 tablespoons minced fresh rosemary

2 tablespoons minced fresh parsley

salt and ground black pepper to taste

⅔ cup chicken broth

⅓ cup butter

1 clove garlic, minced

⅓ medium onion, diced

½ teaspoon salt

¼ teaspoon ground black pepper

⅓ cup all-purpose flour

1 ¾ cups chicken broth

⅔ cup milk

1 8 ounce package frozen mixed vegetables, thawed

aluminum foil

Directions:

- Preheat the oven to 425 °F (220 °C).
- Place 1 pie crust in a 9-inch pie plate. Poke several holes in the bottom of the crust.
- Bake crust in the preheated oven for 5 minutes. Remove and set aside to cool.
- Heat oil in a medium skillet over medium-high heat. Season both sides of chicken breasts with rosemary, parsley, salt, and pepper. Add chicken to the skillet and saute until golden brown, 2 to 4 minutes per side.
- Reduce heat to medium-low and add ⅔ cup chicken broth. Simmer, being careful not to overcook, just until chicken juices run clear, 10 to 15 minutes. Transfer chicken to a plate, allowing it to cool until the juices settle, about 15 minutes. Reserve pan drippings.
- Meanwhile, melt butter in a large skillet over medium heat. Add pan drippings and garlic. Saute until garlic is fragrant, about 30 seconds. Add onion, salt, and pepper and cook until onion is translucent, about 5 minutes. Whisk in flour until mixture thickens.
- Add 1¾ cups chicken broth and milk, 1 cup of liquid at a time, whisking constantly. Remove from heat once mixture begins to thicken.
- Cut chicken into bite-sized pieces and mix with thawed vegetables and broth mixture until combined. Pour into the pre-baked pie crust. Cut slits in the remaining pie crust and place it on top of the pie, crimping the edges to seal and decorating them with tongs or a fork, if desired.
- Place pot pie in the oven and bake until crust is golden brown, 30 to 40 minutes. Check edges halfway through baking time and cover them with aluminum foil if they start to brown too much.

Ravven's Ravvings

Dear Ravven,

What is your favorite childhood memory?

My favorite childhood memory is of my brother and I blowing bubbles on our front porch one summer. We were both pretty young but I remember watching the bubbles lazily float through the air, glinting in the sunlight. It was just the two of us and it was peaceful and quiet. To me, it just feels very nostalgic..

What's your favorite movie growing up?

Oooo this is a hard one. My favorite movie for awhile was Disney's Aladdin. My mom says I used to belt out the songs so loud you could clearly hear me in another room. Later on I remember really loving The Little Mermaid and Beauty and The Beast.

What media influenced you most from your childhood?

Hands down video games! I actually have an article about this question here in the issue! I was also really into claymation and animation as well and at one point hoped to become an animation artist in the movie world!

Do you have a favorite pastime from your childhood?

At one point I was obsessed with Sherlock Holmes and wanted to train myself to be as observant as he was and I kept a notebook of 'observations'. I was also really into spies and would pretend to go on missions and I'd write down who I was following and pretend to send it to headquarters. I do the same thing now but I call it being an author...

Favorite childhood snack?

I love the animal crackers with the pink icing and sprinkles! I also really enjoyed rice krispie treats and still do!

Favorite books or series?

I would say when I was still pretty young I enjoyed The Magic Treehouse series, Encyclopedia Brown, and the Mandie series. The Magic Treehouse was literally a magic treehouse that transported to different times and places to teach kids about history. Encyclopedia Brown was pretty much a child Sherlock Holmes and he solved crimes around his neighborhood. Mandie was about a young girl who had lots of adventures and solved mysteries with her friends. It was very wholesome and I'd check out up to five books at a time in the series because I read them so fast!

Looking for your next favorite?
Maddy's
Needful Reads
Magpie Messenger Spring Equinox 2023

The Pickety Witch
Cute witchy things
Online & across the country.

Pride

Ravven White

TW: Homophobia

As the founder of a small press, I consider it my duty to use my platform to enrich the world around me, bring awareness to impactful issues, and create a safe space for conversation. I do this through the content I choose to publish and market, through the people I represent and interact with, and of course how I talk and post on social media. It's a duty that I consider sacred and while I may not have a huge presence online, I take it seriously, nonetheless.

I've made no effort to hide the fact that I publish queer content and host a diverse group of authors either in the community or allies of it. Publishing queer stories is something hugely important to me. One because the LGBTQ+ community is still not represented well or enough. We have queer side characters that are killed off or assigned to a stereotype, bi and lesbian erasure, closeted homophobia, and a general misunderstanding of what it means to be "queer".

For me, it's more personal. I am thirty-two years old and it wasn't until I was almost thirty that I finally found words that described the way I felt and thought.

Because I am queer.

Surprise! *Shocking,* I know. In all seriousness though, why did it take me so long to learn about the LGBTQ+ community? Why was it kept from me? Why was I forced to deal with years and years of isolation and grief–*profound grief*–created from not understanding myself and believing that I was just inherently wrong? I was trapped in this horrible, depressing inner hate because the beliefs and opinions I had been raised in kept me from my true community.

I'm not here to argue with you on personal beliefs or theology. At the end of the day what matters is that I am a human. I am here in front of you with real human problems and real human love and my existence and the existence of those like me is valid. *We are real.*

This lack of access and knowledge has given me a drive to make sure that no one has to experience what I have. That hopefully I can save some people a little bit of time and bring awareness to who and what our community is. Because it's a great one, filled with beautiful people and rich history.

And speaking of history.

In the UK, February is LGBTQ+ history month. Our author, David Turton, is a strong ally of the community and he even wrote a book about the treatment of gay men during World War 2. His book, *The Psychic of Sachsenhausen,* is based on the real life, true to history events of the Sachsenhausen concentration camp, one of the largest gay camps in Nazi Germany. I am ashamed to say that I didn't know this camp even existed prior to David and once again, that lack of knowledge compelled me to make sure this book saw the light of day and reach as many people as possible. It's a gruesome story. It's a necessary reminder.

Racist crap!!

Oh good Lord.

Twisted perverted sick

Bull crap

You lasted a month?? Ha ha

From the deepest of HELL

IDGARA

In honor of the month, I decided to run a $.99 eBook sale and advertised it on Facebook and Instagram. The ad contained the synopsis of the book, a photo of the cover, a brief overview of LGBTQ+ history month, and where the book could be found. What followed was an onslaught of homophobic hate and bigotry. It got so bad that I ended up deleting the entire ad because I could not cope with the vicious and terrible comments.

It was the first time I had dealt with hate comments and messages telling me to kill myself. I realized I had been very sheltered in Curious Corvid for our first two years and it absolutely broke my heart that people could be so hateful on a post about a book.

I decided to regroup. I took screenshots of some of the 'less' hateful comments and created an ad to showcase why queer books are so important. I specifically targeted the LGBTQ+ community, hoping to reach the right people. Once again, I instead received a barrage of hateful and derogatory comments and opinions. They continued until the ad reached its finish.

LGBT are you Kidd me. Ugh.

I agree with all the above commenters...thank you for boldly declaring what you truly believe about such nonsense...

LG/ HDTV

Going straight to hell

I'm not going to lie. The first thing I felt was grief and anger and a lot of fear. Fear that no matter what I did, I was going to continue to receive messages and comments. Anger because what was happening wasn't fair and no one was out there stopping it. And grief because it's hard to believe that after so much time and so much history, there is still such backwards and uneducated thoughts surrounding the LGBTQ+ people.

Because we are people. We are as real as the people writing the comments. We are as real as the legislators passing harmful laws. And somehow, our realness gets replaced with fear and ill meaning beliefs.

What transpired in February changed me. I have not felt the same since. A friend of mine made the remark that I would have to get used to this because this is the life I have chosen. That is only half true.

My choice has never involved the harm or hate towards another person. And it is unfair that any queer person has to live their life in fear of retaliation just for simply existing. We deserve more than that.

I would like to kindly ask that if you have ever felt like the LGBTQ+ community was being shoved in your face or down your throat, or if you don't understand why we have events like Pride, you take a moment to think on my shared experience. And mine is so small in comparison to what happens to many of my queer brothers and sisters, specifically my trans siblings in the current political climate. We have our parades and celebrations to remind people that we are real. That we exist. That we have had to fight and scream and bleed for the representation we have, for the rights we so desperately cling to, for the ability to walk in the streets and come home to our families. And every day, there are people hellbent on taking it away from us, happy to watch us disappear.

Representation matters. Queer books matter. *We* matter.

And clearly, our work is far from done. If you are part of our community I just want you to know: I see you. I hear you. I love you. And I promise to continue to use my platform to bring awareness, conversation, inclusion, and hope.

Together, we can do better. We have to.

Curious Corvid
PUBLISHING
CUSTOM T-SHIRT
100% COTTON
Curious Corvid
PUBLISHING
CUSTOM T-SHIRT
100% COTTON
UNIQUE
GOTHIC
STYLE.
Check out our store for unique merch and gifts
in addition to our written works.

Become a Member of our Murder

Members of Curious Corvid enjoy a variety of perks, from early access sneak peeks, to special sales, to lots and lots of additional content. Membership is free—we just want to connect with you. Join a community that breaks the mold of the traditional publishing industry, and discover new ways to engage you won't find at other publishing houses.

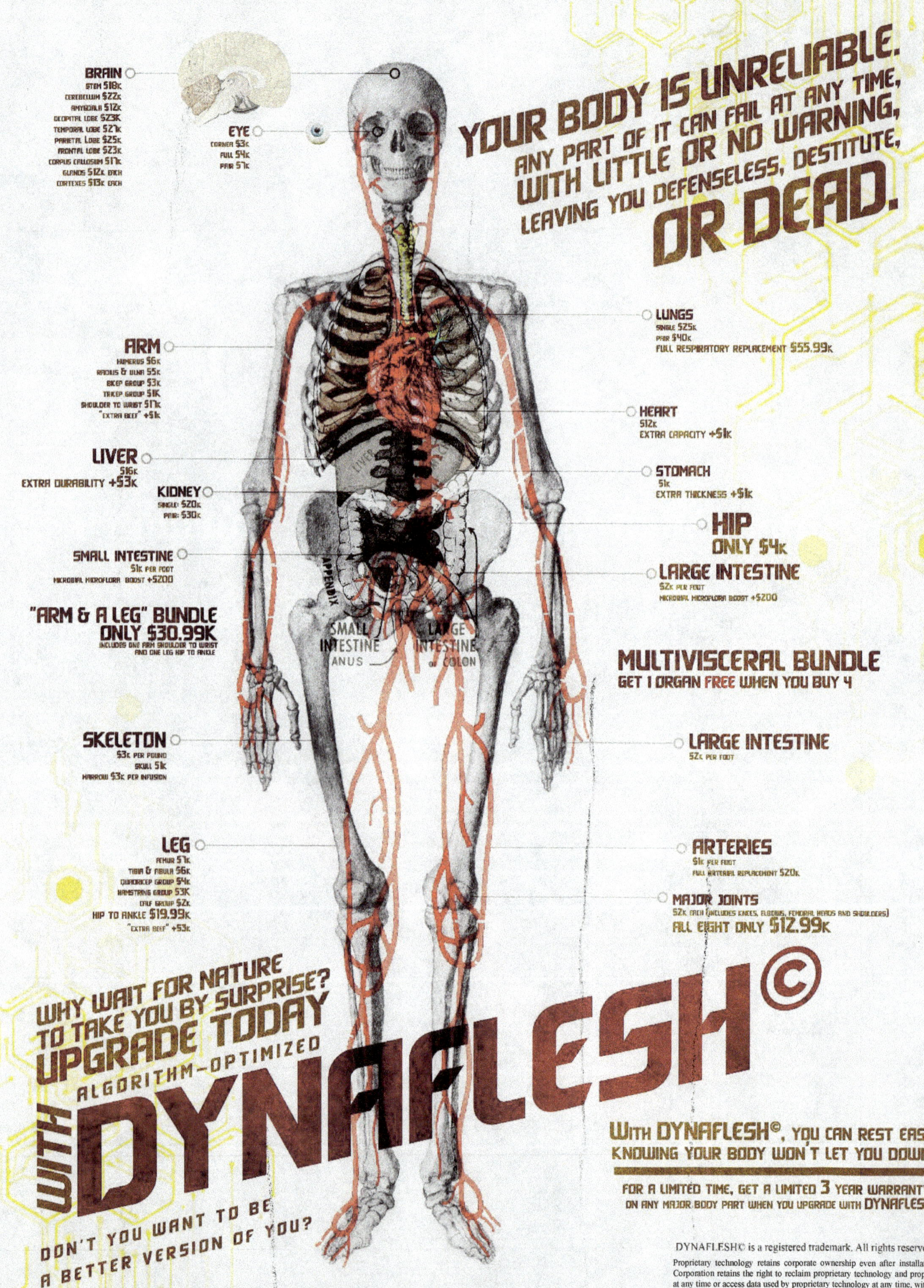

YOUR BODY IS UNRELIABLE.
ANY PART OF IT CAN FAIL AT ANY TIME,
WITH LITTLE OR NO WARNING,
LEAVING YOU DEFENSELESS, DESTITUTE,
OR DEAD.

BRAIN
STEM $18k
CEREBELLUM $22k
AMYGDALA $12k
OCCIPITAL LOBE $23k
TEMPORAL LOBE $27k
PARIETAL LOBE $25k
FRONTAL LOBE $23k
CORPUS CALLOSUM $17k
GLANDS $12k EACH
CORTEXES $13k EACH

EYE
CORNEA $3k
FULL $4k
PAIR $7k

LUNGS
SINGLE $25k
PAIR $40k
FULL RESPIRATORY REPLACEMENT $55.99k

ARM
HUMERUS $6k
RADIUS & ULNA $5k
BICEP GROUP $3k
TRICEP GROUP $1k
SHOULDER TO WRIST $17k
"EXTRA BEEF" +$1k

HEART
$12k
EXTRA CAPACITY +$1k

LIVER
$16k
EXTRA DURABILITY +$3k

KIDNEY
SINGLE $20k
PAIR $30k

STOMACH
$1k
EXTRA THICKNESS +$1k

HIP
ONLY $4k

SMALL INTESTINE
$1k PER FOOT
MICROBIAL MICROFLORA BOOST +$200

LARGE INTESTINE
$2k PER FOOT
MICROBIAL MICROFLORA BOOST +$200

"ARM & A LEG" BUNDLE
ONLY $30.99k
INCLUDES ONE ARM SHOULDER TO WRIST
AND ONE LEG HIP TO ANKLE

APPENDIX

SMALL
INTESTINE
ANUS

LARGE
INTESTINE
OR COLON

MULTIVISCERAL BUNDLE
GET 1 ORGAN FREE WHEN YOU BUY 4

SKELETON
$3k PER POUND
SKULL $1k
MARROW $3k PER INFUSION

LARGE INTESTINE
$2k PER FOOT

LEG
FEMUR $7k
TIBIA & FIBULA $6k
QUADRICEP GROUP $4k
HAMSTRING GROUP $3k
CALF GROUP $2k
HIP TO ANKLE $19.99k
"EXTRA BEEF" +$3k

ARTERIES
$1k PER FOOT
FULL ARTERIAL REPLACEMENT $20k

MAJOR JOINTS
$2k EACH (INCLUDES KNEES, ELBOWS, FEMORAL HEADS AND SHOULDERS)
ALL EIGHT ONLY $12.99k

WHY WAIT FOR NATURE
TO TAKE YOU BY SURPRISE?
UPGRADE TODAY
ALGORITHM-OPTIMIZED
WITH DYNAFLESH©

DON'T YOU WANT TO BE
A BETTER VERSION OF YOU?

WITH DYNAFLESH©, YOU CAN REST EASY
KNOWING YOUR BODY WON'T LET YOU DOWN.

FOR A LIMITED TIME, GET A LIMITED 3 YEAR WARRANTY
ON ANY MAJOR BODY PART WHEN YOU UPGRADE WITH DYNAFLESH.

DYNAFLESH© is a registered trademark. All rights reserved.

Proprietary technology retains corporate ownership even after installation.
Corporation retains the right to reclaim proprietary technology and property
at any time or access data used by proprietary technology at any time, with or
without notice. Use of proprietary technology implies compliance with all
terms and conditions associated with use.

Born in North Carolina, Dustin Allen Smith has been a writer and avid storyteller most of his adult life.

While attending college, he began work on his first significant piece of writing, *Life of Shadows* (as yet unpublished), and it steered him towards becoming a full-time writer.

DUSTIN ALLEN SMITH

Welcome to the world of *Hart's Dilemma.*

Society is run by The Algorithm.

The Algorithm measures cost-to-benefit ratios and replaces natural organs with artificial organs. While these artificial organs work perfectly, the Algorithm has total control over them.

Artificial eyes become cameras. Hearing aids become microphones.

The Algorithm is always watching.

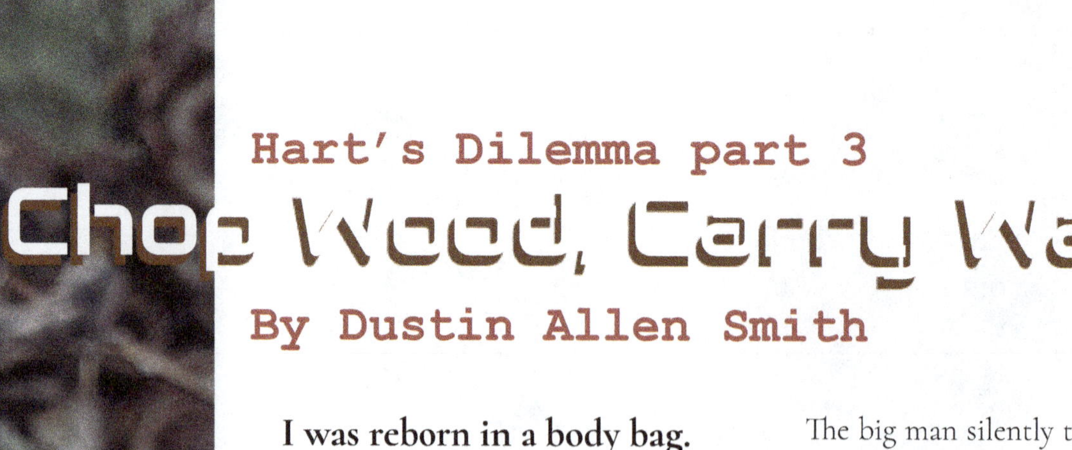

I was reborn in a body bag.

After the girl on the unicycle left me to freeze, I folded my arms and waited on the frosted ground. I shivered uncontrollably but was content that hyperthermia would be one of the less painful ways to die.

A big hand picked up the bag I was in and tossed me into the back of a van. The person up front could be carrying me away to an organ farm, and I had lost the urge to fight. Between the drudgery of the factory job and the false hope of a life with purpose, I felt like I deserved it. Like I was nothing, a bit of trash to be bagged up and carried out. As I was blacking out, the motion of the van rocked me to sleep.

They unzipped my bag in a dank wooden cabin. The place smelled like a summer camp.

"Are they up yet?" I recognized the perky voice of Fey as she bounced into the room.

A thumb pulled my lower eyelid down, and I caught the image of a giant.

"Get a medic in here— they look half frozen."

The big man's voice resonated as he spoke. It was clear he was accustomed to people obeying his orders.

"A medic?" Fey asked with a jovial tone.

The big man silently turned to her and leaned over, glaring directly into her eyes. He had to be a foot or two taller. Silently he just stared until Fey wilted.

"Yeah, I'll get somebody," she answered before running off.

The big man turned back to me and wrapped his giant fingers around my hands, warming them. That's when I saw his pin, a golden globe with an eagle sitting on top of it and an anchor in the background.

"Easy recruit, you're going to be fine. We'll warm you up."

I didn't say anything, just closed my eyes and drifted off.

When I came too, the room was dark. I was on a bunk with Fey who was curled up next to me. She was short, when last I saw her she was at eye level with me, but without her unicycle she was almost half my size.

"You're awake." she whispered, "I was starting to get worried."

I tried to speak, but my throat was dry, "What's going on here?"

"You nearly froze to death," was her answer. "Had to figure out a way to warm you up, and Recon gave me the go-ahead to be your snuggle buddy for the night."

"Snuggle buddy?" I asked.

"Yeah, you're welcome," she said, burying her face into my chest.

I wheezed as I breathed, trying to laugh, but I couldn't. Whoever treated me had wrapped my chest in a bandage and placed the red hart pin on it. I felt safe knowing it was there.

"Who's Recon?" I asked.

Fey clutched me like a stuffed animal she had won at a carnival game. "The boss man, er Ringmaster. He's the one that picked you up from the field. He's okay, but I'd stay on his good side if you want to last long here. He can be a real hard ass sometimes."

"His pin?" I asked, "I've seen it before. I just can't remember where."

"Military pin, pre-unification. Soldiers used to fight each other in real space before the Algorithm secured the UN."

I don't know why, but I reached up and stroked Fey's hair. Something in my gut told me that's what I was supposed to do. She purred, and I relaxed. It was like whatever I was doing was on autopilot. Then my gut twisted, and I started shaking. I felt electricity all over my body. Everywhere except my chest.

The spot above my artificial heart was null, empty. Like the rest of me was a storm of emotion, but the dead place where my real heart should be was a grave.

Fey started snoring, and I was calmed by it.

In the morning, Recon, that giant of a man who ran the circus, woke me.

"Morning recruit, time to rise and shine. I got you some clothes; they're on the chair."

At some point in the night, Fey had woken up and snuck away. Now I was sitting up, trying to figure out what to say next.

"So, what's the plan?"

The big man turned around and displayed a wicked grin.

"Day one— orientation." He lifted an ax with one hand, and I held my breath. Then Recon laughed and flipped it midair, offering me the handle.

"Day one, most important job there is: Chop wood, carry water."

I took the ax, and the head dropped to the floor. Recon stepped out and left me to get dressed.

We passed cabins and a mess hall. There were utility sheds and discarded golf carts.

I was right; it was a summer camp. Made sense— nature was as antithetical to the Algorithm as anything I could think of.

The smell of something burning lingered in the air and I could hear the faint sound of a generator.

"Chop wood, carry water. When in doubt, when you can't think of what to do. Chop wood, carry water. We use wood to cook food, boil water, and make syngas for the generator."

Recon led me through the underbrush, and our heavy coats snagged on saplings and dead bushes.

"You want the dry ones, young trees are too wet they won't catch. You just get a lot of smoke."

He selected the branch on a medium-sized tree and grabbed it, using a hatchet to chip at the bark.

"So," I asked, "What is it we do here?"

Recon paused momentarily, "I told you. We chop wood, carry water."

I nodded instinctively, "Wait, what," I said, snapping out of it, "That's it? That's what the circus does? We will overthrow the Algorithm by chopping wood and carrying water?"

"It's what you do. First things first." He returned to the task.

"Chop wood, carry water."

And that's what I did for months. Chop wood and carry water.

I got blisters. I got splinters. I tripped and fell, but I found peace.

At first, I was awful. Recon stuck with me for the first month till I got the basics down. After the second month, I stopped second-guessing everything and did it as I thought I was supposed to. Then I stopped thinking about it, and it all started to feel natural. After three months, I wasn't much better, but I was stronger. I could work at my own pace, saying whatever the hell I wanted when I wanted to say it. I didn't have to live and die by the clock, eating or pissing at designated hours. Still had to work, but it was my work.

Fey even commented on how I was shaping up during one of our 'Snuggle sessions.'

I got the feeling she was sneaking around to see me. She'd come in the middle of the night and slide into my bunk without saying a word. I knew her by the smell of peaches in Earl Grey tea and how cold her feet were at any time of the night.

There were others— my best guess is 13 people were living at the camp. People would go with me to gather supplies. Sometimes Recon, Oscar, and Whiskey would grab bows and go hunting together.

I remember one day Happy Cat, one of the campers, asked me if I'd ever been on a dive.

"You mean like in the River?" She just laughed and ran off to smoke something rancid.

Three months on the job, three months of peace.

Chop wood, carry water.

Then it all went to pot. I was fast asleep, Fey under my arm, when the alarm went off. So we got up and rushed to the office.

"What's going on," Fey asked. Recon looked us over; the whole cell was there.

He didn't say a word, just gestured for us to follow him.

What I saw shook me hard. Recon's eyes burned into me, waiting for some tell.

I was a nervous wreck, at least, but the mechanical heart in my chest kept beating away at an even keel. It was a piece of the machine, utterly oblivious to how the rest of me was shriveling up.

On the floor, lying in a pool of blood was Oscar. Dead hands were desperately clutching an ax buried in his chest, my ax.

Puzzle Answers

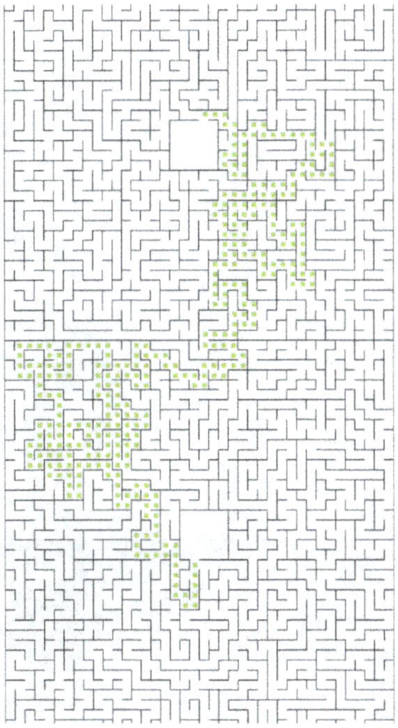

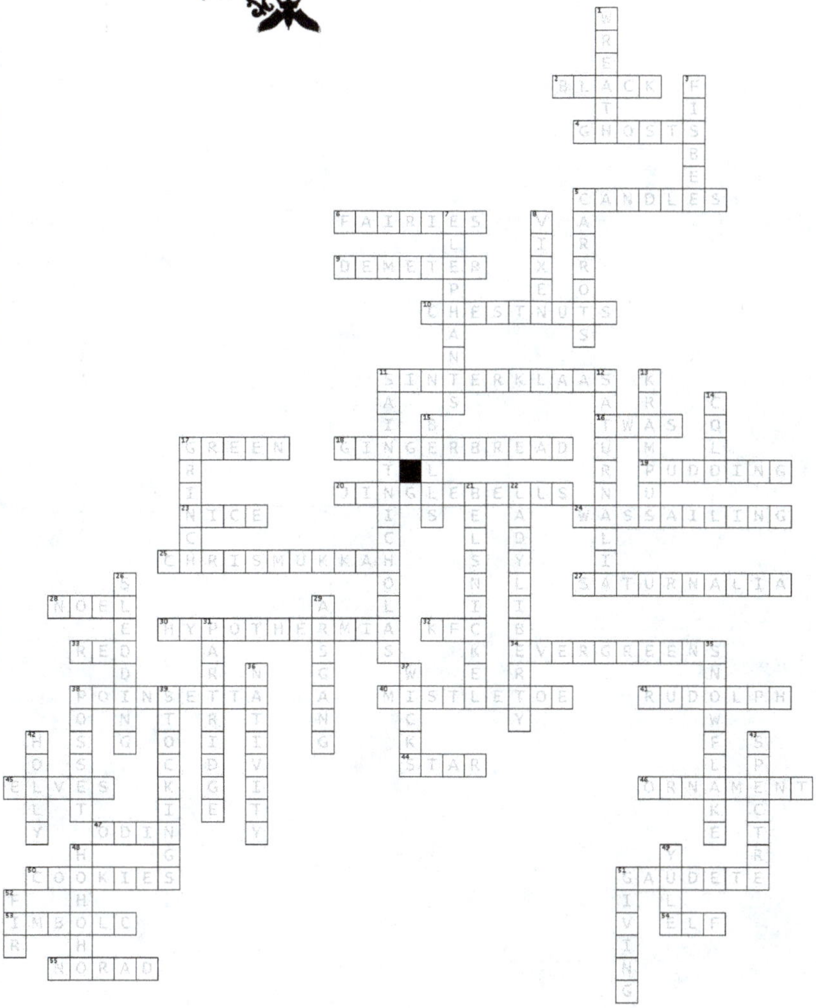

How did we do?

Did you enjoy this issue of the Magpie Messenger? We want to hear your honest feedback. Scan the QR code below for an easy, anonymous survey and help us improve!

Magpie Messenger

curated by Curious Corvid Publishing, LLC

Design & layout by
Mark Alexander McClish

Edited by Ravven White and Aimee Nicole

Graphics and images provided by Freepik, Rawpixel, Pexels, and Vecteezy.

All works used with the authors' express permission.

Printed in the United States of America

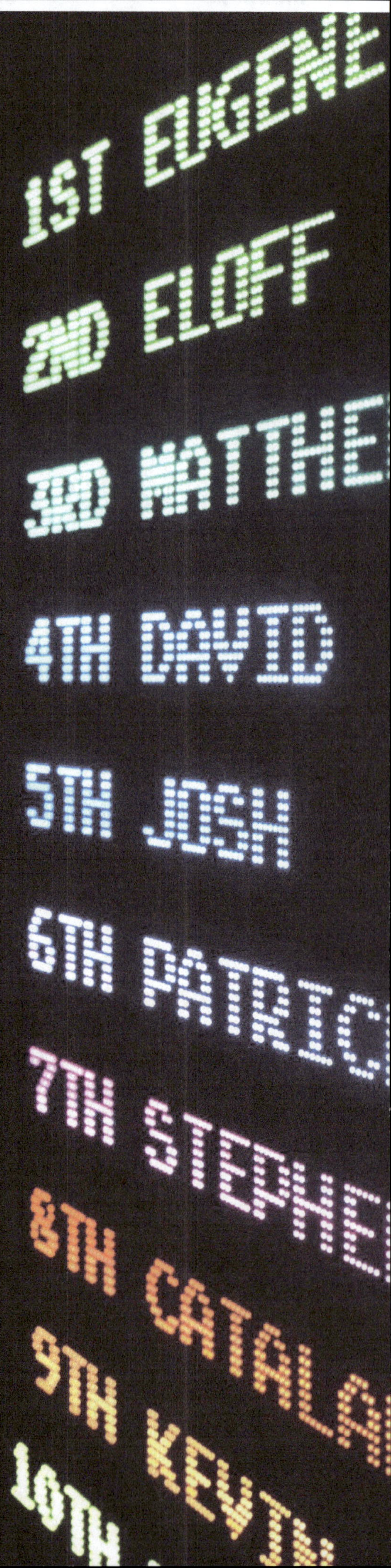

Curious Corvid Publishing

was created to build a home and community for indie creatives who have been left in the shadows. We are passionate about the indie writing community and bringing underrepresented voices and themes to our table. We are proud to represent a diverse group of indie voices that create fresh narratives and compelling stories, bringing uncommon delights to everyone who appreciates them. If you're a little weird, a little dark, and delightfully creative, you'll fit right in with us.